Meigs County, Tennessee

Marriages

1851 – 1865

Byron and Barbara Sistler

Byron Sistler & Associates, Inc.
1988

Notice

In many older books, foxing (or discoloration) occurs and, in some instances, print lightens with wear and age. Reprinted books, such as this, often duplicate these flaws, notwithstanding efforts to reduce or eliminate them. The pages of this reprint have been digitally enhanced and, where possible, the flaws eliminated in order to provide clarity of content and a pleasant reading experience.

Originally published:
Nashville, 1988

Reprinted by:
Janaway Publishing, Inc.
2007, 2012

Janaway Publishing, Inc.
732 Kelsey Ct.
Santa Maria, California 93454
(805) 925-1038
www.janawaygenealogy.com

ISBN: 978-1-59641-128-9

Made in the United States of America

MEIGS COUNTY, TN MARRIAGES

1851-1865

Where two dates appear on an entry, the first one is the date license was issued, the second (in parentheses) the date marriage was solemnized. If only one date, it usually means that the date of execution was the same as the date of license issuance.

Sometimes the execution of the marriage was not reported to the courthouse, and occasionally the clerk failed to note in the marriage book that the license was returned. We would usually make a notation in the entry to indicate the non-execution of a marriage if the book so stated.

The marriages are arranged alphabetically, the first half of the book by groom--the second by bride.

The records included in this book were transcribed by us directly from microfilm of the original marriage books. Error, where it occurs, may be attributed to us, or to the clerks of the period, many of whom did an appallingly sloppy job of entering the information.

If the bride and groom were black, a B is placed at the end of the entry.

It should be remembered that this and other marriage books we have prepared are indexes, and do not include all the information to be found in the original marriage book. Such data as names of bondsmen, ministers, justices of the peace, churches, etc., are omitted. Often such information is helpful to the researcher. Consequently the serious researcher, to obtain this additional information as well as to check on the accuracy of the transcriber, should examine the original marriage record if at all possible.

Byron Sistler
Barbara Sistler

Nashville, TN
January 1988

Marriages Arranged Alphabetically

By

GROOM

Meigs County Grooms

(name illegible), to Polly E. Holingsworth 11-11-1859 (11-12-1859)
Abel, William J. to Malinda H. Guinn 5-21-1850
Ackman?, Jno. S. to Lucy Ann Atchley 9-17-1863
Adams, F. G. to D. E. Blevins 6-15-1863 (6-16-1863)
Adams, James to Harriete Caps 1-20-1849 (1-21-1849)
Adams, W. B. to Rachael Guinn 3-7-1851
Adkins, Sanford to Mary Stanley 1-29-1850
Adkins, Spencer to Eliza Hudson 5-18-1860 (5-20-1860)
Ahart, Geo. W. to Frances Robertson 9-24-1850
Aikman, Wm. F. to Sarah Jane Looney 2-15-1854
Aikman?, James A. to Parle Stone 7-19-1860
Albert, John M. to Eliza M. Golloway 9-4-1845
Alcley?, Miles to Elizabeth Mitchell 7-21-1845
Alexander, William to Melsina McAdams 1-6-1847
Alford, John M. to Hannah Holloman 4-13-1847
Alfred, Arlander D. to Polly Jane Holloman 4-7-1853
Alison, John to Alsia Buckler 11-7-1847
Allen, Ethen to Jennie K. Patterson 12-25-1865 (12-26-1865)
Allen, Isaiah to Naoma Renfroe 12-25-1832
Allen, R. J. D. W. to Lavina McMullen 7-29-1847
Allen, Saml. C. to Jane Wamack 11-5-1861
Allen, W. O. to Matilda Crow 4-29-1856
Allen, William to Delpha Blankenship 7-13-1841
Aller, R. J. D. W. to Elsira Smith 8-24-1857 (8-25-1857)
Aloon?, Noah to Mary J. Francisco 9-1-1845
Armstrong, Wm. T. to Sarah Bell 3-29-1842
Arrants, William to Artemiza Coop 2-13-1845
Ashburn, John to Elizabeth Harrid 10-24-1844
Atchley, Daniel P. to Emeline Jones 1-20-1859 (1-21-1859)
Atchley, Elijah to Lucy Ann Stone 9-27-1859
Atchley, James to Malinda Mahan 12-15-1852
Atchley, James to Tennessee Tillery 6-25-1863 (6-26-1863)
Atchley, John to Rachel Tillerry 7-27-1851
Atchley, Noah to Juda Ann Brooks 10-25-1865 (1-5-1866)
Atchley, Noah R. to Sarah Massengale 10-25-1862 (10-26-1862)
Atchley, P. L. to Elizabeth Hollamon 6-16-1863 (6-17-1863)
Atchley, Robt. to Sarah G.? Powers 6-3-1859 (6-4-1859)
Atchley, Seth to E. M. Francisco 2-18-1840 (3-2?-1840)
Atchley, Wm. to Mahala E. Tillery 1-22-1856
Atchly, Joseph A. to Jane Buster 9-16-1860
Atkinson, Calvin B. to Elizabeth A. Masoner 12-27-1847 (12-30-1847)
Baker, C. to Hulda C. Ledbetter 9-10-1864
Baker, Champanius to Elisabeth Baker 9-30-1847
Baker, Hugh to Caty Eakin 5-21-1840 (6-18-1840)
Baker, James to Sarah E. Wan 11-17-1857 (11-19-1857)
Baker, Jesse to Lucresia Collins 9-14-1853
Baker, John to Nancy Caroline Meadaris 1-9-1850
Baker, Samuel to Polly Renfrow 8-26-1850
Baker, Samuel to Rachel E. Medaris 4-25-1853
Baker, Wilson to Loucinda Jolley 12-20-1850
Baldwin, John L. to Salina Griffith 3-10-1847 (3-11-1847)

1

Meigs County Grooms

Ball, Jno. N. to Elizabeth Rhodes 7-2-1863 (7-3-1863)
Bandy, John W. to Sarah Foar 6-29-1865
Bandy, Reuben E. to Mary Williams 2-15-1840 (2-16-1840)
Bankston, Grimes to Polly Ann Falls 2-17-1844
Bard, henry to Malinda Frie 4-2-1838
Barnhart, Felix to Manervy J. Mckeown 12-18-1845
Barnhart, Henry to Jane Wilson 4-21-1847 (4-22-1847)
Barrett, S. S. to Sarah Hunter 10-16-1865 (10-17-1865)
Barrows, Wm. J. to Caldona E. Lawson 11-24-1863
Beady, James to Lemsea Alfred 9-9-1852
Becknell, George to Jane Paul 6-23-1864
Beeson, Benjamin F. to Sarah F. Gourley 7-16-1844
Bell, James to Dicey Richards 4-8-1854
Bell, Jessey to Minerva Blackwell 2-22-1854
Bennett, David to Liza Jane Lawson 8-25-1854
Bennett, John to Nancy E. Newman 12-6-1864
Benson, John to Melissa Wamack 2-25-1864
Benton, Francis M. to Mary Hudson 7-10-1840 (7-12-1840)
Benton, Lewis to Rebecca Smith 5-28-1849
Benton, Louis to Mary Bishop 12-5-1857
Billings, John to Susan Kitchens 8-5-1865
Binyon, Richard to Nancy E. Woods 11-21-1850
Bishop, Benj. to Serena Isom 1-4-1853
Bishop, Francis to Mythursda Malone 8-26-1851
Bishop, John D. to Malinda Overshultz 12-10-1853
Black, James M. to Vesta M. (Emily?) Green 10-1-1851
Blackwell, Joseph to Emily Blackwell 2-27-1865
Blackwell, William to Eliza Dixon? 3-29-1838
Blalock, Samuel to Elizabeth Murphy 11-24-1851
Blankenship, John to Susanna Lawson 5-24-1854
Blankenship, Wallas to Martha Bennet 11-6-1860
Blankenship, Wm. to Martha J. Barnett 9-15-1853
Blankenship, Wm. W. to Polina Armstrong 11-11-1857
Blanton, Thomas to Mahalia Homes 3-2-1839 (3-7-1839)
Blaylock, E. P. to Sarah A. Blaylock 1-28-1865
Blaylock, S. H. to M. A. Blaylock 10-25-1857
Blevens, Philip to Harriet Blakely 12-6-1838
Blevins, Anderson to Caroline Quiett 12-30-1847 (8-7-1848)
Blevins, Harrison to Nancy Blevins 11-23-1848
Blevins, Moses to Elizabeth Thomas 8-27-1839 (8-29-1839)
Blevins, Philip M. to Altamyra Shears 9-5-1858
Blevins, Res. to Amanda E. Blevins 5-25-1851
Blevins, Thos. to Levina P. Gorley 6-13-1839 (7-1-1839)
Bly, Samuel to Franky Raby 12-25-1865 (12-28-1865)
Blythe, James to Mary Tuck 6-7-1854
Blythe, John to Mary Ann Murphy 11-18-1854
Blythe, William to Marthey Bayless 11-12-1849
Boggess, Abijah to Levina Sharp 2-3-1851
Boggess, J. H. to Mahala R. Neil 1-31-1859 (2-3-1859)
Boggess, John B. to Mary A. Lillard 8-1-1850
Bolen, Wm. to Elizabeth A. Johnson 12-13-1863
Bolin, William to Polly M. Richards 10-29-1848

Meigs County Grooms

Boll, William J. to Nancy Ann Cofer 8-30-1860 (9-2-1860)
Bonner, E. to R. J. Martin 4-4-1860 (4-5-1860)
Bonner, Thomas G. to Elizabeth J. Howser 7-16-1861 (7-17-1861)
Bonner, Thomas G. to Susanah Wamack 3-21-1859
Bonner, Thomas J. to Sarah Wammack 9-5-1850
Bourk?, William to Malinda McClenahan 5-9-1838
Bowers, Newton to Magdaline Curtain 9-12-1861 (9-15-1861)
Bowling, Thomas to Eliza J. Reed 11-2-1862
Boyd, Martin L. to Martha E. Pierce 3-5-1856
Bracket, Morgan to Elizabeth Mayfield 11-4-1841
Bracket, William to Eliza J. Gilbreath 10-21-1845 (10-22-1845)
Brackett, William to Rebecca J. Milloway? 9-21-1858 (9-30-1858)
Brackett, Wm. to Betsy Ann Milloway 12-14-1856
Brackins, Alfred to Margaret McCoy 1-2-1841 (1-3-1841)
Bradey, Levy to Nancy Green 12-22-1841 (12-25-1841)
Brandon, John to Mary Sutherland 7-?-1858 (7-1-1858)
Branham, Gideon to Sarah Jan Alford 10-6-1859
Braziel, Larcum to Mary Braziel 2-9-1854
Briggs, James to Mary Fooshee 4-10-1850
Brightwell, Elgin to Eliza Armstrong 8-19-1843 (8-20-1843)
Brightwell, Gainum to Nancy Walker 12-29-1839
Brightwell, Jefferson to Mahaley Armstrong 3-21-1858 (3-23-1858)
Brighwell, Elgin to Mary Jane Houser 10-24-1850
Brighwell, Gainum to Nancy Houser 9-24-1850
Brison, Wm. to Rebecca Davis 8-31-1856
Brogden, Franklin to Isabella Davis 6-24-1856
Brogden, Wm. W. to Mary E. Murphey 11-29-1859
Broiles, Amos to Clarrinza L. Wilson 7-1-1845
Brooks, A. J. to Mary Ann Worick 1-9-1845 (1-12-1845)
Brooks, John to Rebeca Hall 5-30-1840 (5-31-1840)
Brooks, Leonard to Margaret Kith? 12-23-1841
Brooks, Z. F. to Angeline Miller 2-16-1856
Browden, James to Louisa E. Childress 12-19-1843
Browder, Albert to Gemina Matlock 12-21-1846 (12-24-1846)
Brown, Cager Jackson to Mary Adaline Mawin 5-8-1854
Brown, Columbus to Harret Lawrence 10-21-1851
Brown, John M. to Sarah Johnson 12-10-1855
Brown, Joseph to Cynthia Lankford 1-21-1858
Brown, Richard to Luvena Lewis 12-15-1848 (12-16-1848)
Broyles, Miles M. to Eleanor C. Wilson 5-20-1845
Bryan, Morgan to Belinda Gibson 12-11-1851
Buckner, Burrow to Lousey Hale 4-17-1858 (4-18-1858)
Buckner, James to Sarah C. Martin 10-4-1858
Bumham, Barba Towsa to Mary Isley James Correll 1-30-1851
Bunch, Benjamon to Ruthy Carrell 6-19-1858 (6-26-1858)
Bunch, Greenberry to Sidney C. Kuntz 4-27-1859 (4-28-1859)
Bunch, Joseph to Abby J. Falls 9-27-1859 (9-28-1859)
Bunch, Paul to Leter Brighwell 2-3-1851
Bunch, Paul to Mahalda Goforth 12-22-1849 (12-23-1849)
Burcham, James to Katharine Thompson 3-3-1847 (3-4-1847)
Burchfield, James to Mary Oleinger 9-15-1860 (9-16-1860)
Burgess, James to Sarah Hosuer 1-14-1851

Meigs County Grooms

Burley, James to Luovina Pettitt 7-15-1843
Buster, Jacob to Malisy Rothwell 10-17-1860
Buster, Michael W. to Elizabeth Wan 12-24-1845 (12-25-1845)
Buster, Saml. to M. A. Royster 8-13-1839 (8-18-1839)
Buster, William to Matilda Guinn 12-31-1846
Buster, Wm. to Nancy Price 1-17-1839 (1-20-1839)
Butler, A. H. to Louisa Gibson 10-21-1857 (10-22-1857)
Butler, Isaac to Rachel Watson 10-2-1857 (11-2-1857)
Butler, J. M. to Hariet G. Johnson 4-7-1845
Butler, Jacob J. to Matilda Gibson 11-28-1849 (11-29-1849)
Butler, James to Malinda Rouden 5-29-1844
Butten, Isac to Martha Price 12-26-1851
Buttram, Elzy to Susan Locke 9-2-1847
Buttram, Larkin to Rebecca Hamilton 2-27-1856
Calbough, John to Betsy Shiply 12-15-1851
Calbough, Nathan to Rosana Long 2-15?-1860
Campbell, Andrew to Sarah Shiflett 11-10-1840 (11-12-1840)
Campbell, James M. to Margaret J. Gamble 1-18-1847 (1-21-1847)
Campbell, John B. to Caroline McClanahan 1-21-1846
Cantrell, J. P. W. to M. E. Myers 3-16-1863 (3-19-1863)
Carter, James to Emily Atkinson 9-1-1843
Carter, Jesse to Martha L. Matthews 9-20-1858
Carter, John E. to Prudence Johnson 10-20-1857 (10-22-1857)
Casey, Isaac J. to Emily E. Farmer 6-13-1858 (6-17-1858)
Casey, Wm. to Sarah A. Locke ?-?-1850
Cash, Benjamin to Louisa Rodis 3-18-1846 (3-19-1846)
Cash, Hugh to Leane Murphy 12-21-1854
Cash, John G. to Adaline Moore 8-4-1847
Cash, Ruben to Mary Jane Jackson 5-23-1853
Cate, A. B. to Sarah Witt 1-22-1860
Cate, Alfred to Nancy Thomas 8-14-1845
Cate, George W. to Catharine Vaughn 3-27-1864
Cate, Samuel A. to Eliza Benton 3-26-1865
Cawood, Thomas to Ruth Ford 12-22-1841 (12-25-1841)
Cawood, Thos. to Sarah Ford 1-5-1854
Chambers, Daniel W. to Sarah Coffey 10-14-1843
Chapman, John to Kisiah Iseral 5-23-1855
Chastian, Jonathan K. to Jane L. Stone 8-21-1843
Chattin, E. R. to M. E. Todd 12-3-1849 (12-5-1849)
Childres, Wm. to Nancy Shewbird 9-17-1853
Childress, Wm. to Minerva Welsh 4-11-1863 (4-12-1863)
Childress, Wm. to Sophia Taylor 9-19-1841
Childress, Wm. M. to Lidia Ann Stanly 11-13-1841
Choate, Henderson to Elizabeth Martin 11-28-1862
Clack, Wiley B. to Sarah Davis 11-28-1852
Clark, Abraham to Maryann Edgman 11-9-1840 (11-12-1840)
Clark, John A. to Lousanna Edgemon 11-22-1843 (11-23-1843)
Clark, Marion Columbus to Sarah Catharine Locke 12-14-1861 (12-15-18
Clementson, G. M. to Sarah Ann Sharp 10-28-1854
Clemons, John to Susannah Mavity 7-8-1845
Clerk, Daniel M. to Ammey Mardy Molton 9-17-1849 (9-20-1849)
Click, G. W. to Mary Hughs 4-4-1839

Meigs County Grooms

Cliften, John to E. R. Sadler 12-31-1843
Cofer, John to Nancy J. Shiflet 7-30-1845
Cofer, John to Nancy J. Shiflett 7-30-1845
Cofer, Joseph to Mary Ann Shiflet 7-28-1842
Coffey, Leven S. to Celia Perry 12-24-1844
Coffey, Michael W. to Anna Williams 4-6-1842 (4-7-1842)
Colbaugh, George to Jane Brogdon 3-9-1865
Colbaugh, John to Nancy McAdoo 8-20-1855
Colbaugh, Nathan to Lucinda Jane Jenkins 2-17-1855
Cole, John to Sophia A. Burcham 6-18-1844 (6-20-1844)
Collins, Enoch to Elizabeth Wasson 7-28-1849 (8-9-1849)
Collins, Henry to Martha A. Powers 3-16-1864 (3-24-1864)
Collins, James E. to Charlotte Kincannon 2-15-1862 (2-16-1862)
Collins, James E. to Jane Rigg 9-13-1843 (9-14-1843)
Collins, Jonathan M. to Caroline Royster 1-27-1849 (1-28-1849)
Collins, Joseph to Elender McDaniel 11-6-1850
Collins, Joseph to Susan Hymes 8-2-1864
Collins, Joseph L. to Rebecca Sewell 11-30-1852
Collins, Reubin C. to Elizabeth C. Lock 8-17-1849 (8-18-1849)
Collins, Troy F. to Mariah Bunch 4-17-1855
Collins, William to Ailsey Harp 4-29-1856
Collins, Wm. to Catharine Blevins 1-16-1851
Collins, Wm. to Elisa Jane Young 10-15-1849
Colvin, Eli to Dinely Rogers 7-11-1846
Colwell, Isaac to Nancy Ramsey 6-2-1853
Conduff, Isaac H. to Mary Fitch 12-25-1851
Conner, Maximillian to Margaret C. Gross 1-2-1855
Cookson, Isaac to Martha Moreland 4-15-1848
Cooley, John to Catharine Clanahan 10-14-1851
Cooley, John to Jane McClanahan 11-8-1860
Cooley, Philip to Mary Newman 4-29-1863
Copeland, VanBuren to Sarah Thomas 4-7-1854
Corder, Sylvester to Jane Price 9-27-1864
Corder, Sylvester to Sarah Jane Price 12-30-1864
Correll, Alexander to Elizabeth Rice 8-14-1851
Correll, James to Emaline Rowden 11-1-1856
Correll, Wm. M. to Lockey Rice 9-15-1854
Corvin, James to Sarah Martin 8-21-1845 (8-25-1845)
Corvin, Philo to Lidda Myres 11-18-1857 (11-24-1857)
Corvin, Philow to Lidda Myres 11-18-1857
Corvin, Philow to Peggy Teague 2-7-1845 (2-10-1845)
Corvin, William to Adaline Corvin 6-14-1865
Cosby, John W. to Angenire Lewis 12-17-1850
Cote, Joseph H. to Margaret Tillery 9-1-1842
Cowan, James A. to Jane Collins 7-24-1844 (7-25-1844)
Cox, Andrew to Matilda Cox 7-26-1865 (7-27-1865)
Cox, Edward F. to Sarah Ann Cox 8-16-1851
Cox, John to Mary Ann Scott 2-16-1848 (8-7-1848)
Cox, John M. to Susan Russell 12-1-1851
Cox, L. B. to Kitha Bower 10-23-1843 (10-24-1843)
Cox, Thomas to Mary Smith 3-19-1847
Coxey, John to Milly Jane Marshall 1-15-1856

Meigs County Grooms

Crabtree, Jefferson to Emily Blackwell 11-1-1862
Craighead, Alcander A. B. to Margaret Forsythe 4-19-1856
Cranfield, Martin to Manervy Presswood 7-12-1860
Cranfill, Thomas to Mary Price 6-21-1863
Crisp, Elias to Mary Walding 9-3-1838 (9-9-1838)
Cronville, William to Tennessee Low 1-19-1861
Cross, A. L. to Sarah E. Godsey 11-26-1863
Cross, Isaac to Mary Taylor 11-24-1853
Cross, Reece B. to Harriet Cox 2-10-1850
Crossland, Thomas E. to Mary C. Casey 7-4-1846 (7-9-1846)
Crow, Demsey to Lucinda Hail 6-11-1840
Crudgington, Wm. to Nancy Pharriss? 5-13-1838
Cuningham, William A. to Elizabeth J. Armstrong 8-5-1858
Cunningham, James to Catharine J. Forde 5-2-1861 (5-5-1861)
Cunningham, James to Pernado Blankenship 2-14-1855
Cunningham, Martin to Martha Sullivan 1-25-1844
Curtin, Isaac to Harriet Baker 2-7-1854
Curton, Henry L. to Viney Muncy 6-9-1856
Dabney, James to Matilda Haynes 10-7-1851
Dake, Philip M. to Elizabeth Adams 10-13-1853
Daniel, Hankins to Mary Ann Reace 10-7-1851
Davis, Adam to Elizabeth M. Casey 2-23-1853
Davis, Hilliogabinous to Lousa Young 9-16-1853
Davis, J. A. to Mary Spradlin 1-13-1859 (1-14-1859)
Davis, John to Martha Stokes 5-29-1856
Davis, John to Polly Adams 12-19-1840
Davis, John H. to Margaret J. McAdoo 12-11-1850
Davis, John N. to Mary A. McKinson? 12-30-1862
Davis, Philip to MSary McAdams 4-24-1840 (4-26-1840)
Davis, Pleasant H. to Elizabeth A. Atkinson 3-20-1856
Davis, Robert R. to Hariet C. Boggess 10-31-1843 (11-2-1843)
Davis, Samuel to Phebe Harvey 11-5-1842 (11-6-1842)
Davis, T. A. to Mary Adams 9-6-1865
Davis, W. R. to Mary A. Gamble 2-22-1860
Davis, William to Elizabeth Bennett 9-10-1845
Dean, John J. to Mary Clingan 7-1-1864 (7-3-1864)
Dean, P. J. to Sarah C. Starnes 12-22-1843 (12-24-1843)
Dearmon, John to Martha Hunter 4-2-1851
Dearmon, Wm. H. to Susan Rice 6-29-1847 (7-1-1847)
Deatherige, Samuel to Sarah A. Read 7-6-1850
Defriese, Jno. M. to Sarah Jane Gilbraith 9-23-1865 (9-24-1865)
Defriese, Thos. J. to Martha J. Grigsby 6-5-1854
Dempsey, David C. to Maryann Porter 9-12-1842
Dennis, Henry H. to Sarah A. Lane 8-9-1864 (8-11-1864)
Denton, Abraham to Sarah E. Neil 3-27-1865 (3-29-1865)
Derrick?, Jesse to Jan T. Wren? 6-25-1838 (6-20?-1838)
Dobbs, Jesse W. to Margret Colvin 8-30-1845 (9-3-1845)
Dobson, Robert to Emeline Matthews 7-12-1861 (7-14-1861)
Dodson, John W. to Elisabeth Sherman 1-31-1865
Dolin, Josiah to Elisebeth J. Howard 10-22-1857
Dotson, Abner to Susan Hembree 7-28-1846
Doughty, James to Margaret I. Taff 5-19-1854

Meigs County Grooms

Douglass, J. R. to Caroline C. Bottoms 12-9-1847
Drake, N. to Melvina Cooke 5-31-1863 (6-14-1863)
Draper, Thomas to Emaly M. McCallen 10-28-1852
Duckworth, James to Sarah E. McNabb 17-17-1864
Duckworth, John to Elizabeth A. Fooshee 11-7-1863 (11-8-1863)
Duckworth, W. J. to Irena Tillery 5-8-1864
Duckworth, William to Nancy Fooshee 8-9-1851
Duckworth, Wm. to Polly Hill 3-7-1839
Durham, John to Charity Dien 9-6-1851
Eakin, Andrew to Mary Ann Fitch 11-13-1850
Eaves, Thomas J. to Matilda J. Dearman 12-18-1841 (12-19-1841)
Eaves, Wm. to Sarah Blankenship 7-12-1855
Eawin, William to Matilda T. Paine 7-20-1848 (7-23-1848)
Edds, John K. to Prudy Ann Pierce 3-27-1845
Edds, Moses H. to Sariah Peirce 9-24-1849 (9-25-1849)
Edds, Wm. P. to Maria Knight 1-25-1840
Edgeman, Kimball to Kisiah Philips 10-15-1855
Edgemon, Thomas to Glopha Clark 7-21-1842
Edgman, Pollard to Lucinda Philip 3-7-1859 (3-22-1859)
Edwards, Justice to Elizabeth Hufner 10-27-1838 (10-28-1838)
Elder, J. F. to Mary A. Denton 8-2-1858 (8-3-1858)
Elderd, Wm. B. to Mary Kinnum 10-23-1844 (10-24-1844)
Ellis, John L. to Sarah F. Benson 7-11-1850
Elsay, Thomas to Elender A. Tillery 9-16-1840 (9-17-1840)
Emmert, Jacob S. to Lousa McDaniel 6-25-1853
Erwin, Isaac R. to Ann Runyan 11-24-1860 (11-29-1860)
Erwin, William R. to Ava Runyan 11-24-1860 (11-27-1860)
Fairchild, Albert to Vina Newman 12-11-1864
Falls, Owen to Patience Kennedy 9-14-1864
Falls, Thomas to Narcisis Mathews 8-20-1857
Farbank, Wm. to Sarah Ramsey 1-26-1839 (2-1-1839)
Faris, Leander to Martha Brown 7-13-1850
Farless, Martin to Mary Bunch 11-30-1843
Farless, William to Martha Howard 3-13-1862 (3-14-1862)
Farmer, Andrew to Susan Hagen 9-19-1838 (9-20-1838)
Farmer, Aquilla to Mary T. Ford 5-24-1845 (5-25-1845)
Farmer, Thomas S. to Eleanor J. McCollon 1-24-1842 (1-27-1842)
Ferguson, Wm. H. to Elizabeth A. Johnson 11-24-1863
Fikes, James E. to Elizabeth Fooshee 10-7-1845 (10-9-1845)
Fisher, John H. to Nancy E. Owen 10-13-1860 (10-14-1860)
Fitch, Jacob to Barbara L. Shipley 12-10-1864
Fitch, James to Edy Tally 1-13-1846
Fitch, John to Edy W. Fitch 3-9-1847
Fitch, Thomas to Catharine Fitch 10-12-1865
Fitch, William to Elizabeth J. Philips 8-4-1847
Fitzgerald, Alfred to Mart E. Francisco 1-21-1854
Floyd, James J. to Lovisa J. Richards 9-16-1848 (9-17-1848)
Floyd, Mardica to Rebecca Starns 10-30-1852
Fooshee, Geo. to Marthy Paul 8-2-1851
Fooshee, M. to Sarah Barnett 1-22-1859 (1-27-1859)
Foosher, George to Nancy F. Bagwell 5-22-1857 (5-25-1857)
Ford, Frederic H. to Elizabeth Pearce 10-16-1841

Meigs County Grooms

Ford, James to Elnoa Hammons 12-21-1854
Ford, James M. to Celia A. Wood 4-25-1853
Ford, John to Elenor Elison 10-24-1849 (10-25-1849)
Ford, Squire to Elisabeth Floyd 9-30-1848 (10-1-1848)
Ford, Wm. B. to Agnes Butler 3-10-1841
Forde, Edman to Nermawey Law Rence 1-27-1851
Foster, Samuel to Lucy Blaylock 7-20-1852
Foster, Wm. to Mary Locke 3-29-1865 (3-30-1865)
Fox, Andrew to Narcissa Ginett 2-4-1846
Fox, James to Elizabeth Ramsey 2-19-1846
Fox, John to Attanzana Armstrong 1-28-1851
Franklin, Charles to L. Buster 8-17-1839 (9-3-1839)
Franks, James to Sariah Green 9-17-1849 (9-20-1849)
Frazier, A. W. to M. J. Craighead 9-1-1858 (9-2-1858)
Frazur, Besiah to Louisa E. Lillard 9-1-1858
Frew?, B. M. to Edith S. Richards 7-17-1862
Fry, John to Betsey Jones 8-13-1856
Fullington, David to Rebeca Blyth 5-3-1851
Fullington, Gene to Elizabeth Miller? 8-7-1838
Fullington, Geo. to Eliza Butler 8-7-1893
Furbunks, M. to Peggy Hurt 7-16-1839 (7-18-1839)
Furguson, Rufus to N. J. Barmon 11-19-1849 (11-20-1849)
Gaddy, George W. to Sarah Moore 6-19-1858 (6-24-1858)
Gallaher, Pleasant to Elizabeth Bledsoe 8-9-1863
Gallion, Wm. Z. to Elizabeth Simpson 7-25-1853
Gamble, Charles to Martha E. Mason 7-12-1856
Gamble, Charles to Nancy A. Reed 2-17-1847 (2-18-1847)
Gamble, Robert S. to Permelie E. Tilley 1-25-1859
Gant, Thomas M. to Matilda Huff 9-28-1857
Gardner, John to Pheba Davis 6-17-1849
Gaskey, W. J. to Elizabeth Harpe 2-20-1849
Gemore?, Wm. R. to Celia B. Sims 7-6-1864 (7-7-1864)
Genow, Franklin to Catharine Moore 8-2-1848 (8-3-1848)
George, James M. to Telitha C. Rowden 10-30-1855
George, John C. to Mary Wammack 8-31-1850
Gibson, Alford to Sarah Baker 3-11-1842 (3-13-1842)
Gibson, Nicholas to Rebecca Lock 8-18-1848 (8-20-1848)
Gibson, Wiley to Mahaly Edington 5-22-1851
Gibson, Wm. E. to Elizabeth C. Hague 9-11-1842
Gilbert, Edwin D. to Nancy J. Cox 12-19-1854
Givens, Nicholas G. to Martha Jane Moon 12-19-1855
Goddard, Hugh to Martha W. Winton 11-16-1847 (11-6?-1847)
Godsey, Abraham I. to Margaret Collins 2-1-1851
Godsey, Ishmael A. to Emaline Cox 6-15-1847
Godsey, Wm. to Julia Thomas 12-18-1840 (12-21-1840)
Gorley, Saml. to Emily J. L. Melton 6-28-1839 (6-30-1839)
Gourley, John to Lisa Blevins 11-19-1857
Gourley, Samuel H. to Delisa Caril 7-16-1844
Gourley, Wm. P. to Katharine Ellis 3-14-1843
Gourly, Jno. D. to Sarah Jane Blevins 1-6-1859
Gray, William J. to Lydia Burton 5-23-1838 (7-2-1838)
Greaves, James to Nancy Moore 4-13-1858 (5-22-1858)

Meigs County Grooms

Green, John L. to Phereby Newkirk 9-19-1842 (9-20-1842)
Greene, William L. to Lucinda Maloney 12-30-1865 (12-31-1865)
Gregory, Green C. M. to Katharine Hill 1-9-1846 (1-21-1846)
Gregory, Thomas to Narcissus Curtain? 11-30-1861 (12-3-1861)
Gresham, Calloway to Rebecca S. Thompson 8-16-1845 (8-17-1845)
Gresham, James W. to Clara Elder 10-19-1865
Gresham, Wm. to Nancy Witt 9-13-1856
Grey, Aron to Racheal Emory 9-19-1857 (9-21-1857)
Grice, James N. to Nancy Mavity 7-6-1842 (7-8-1842)
Griffen, William to Elizabeth Harvey 9-18-1843 (9-19-1843)
Griffin, Anderson to Iseller Ann Griffin 7-23-1842 (7-24-1842)
Griffin, Jas. to Acilla A. Daniel 3-17-1840
Griffith, John E. to Mary S. Arehart 8-4-1856
Grigsby, Benjamin F. to Mary Ann Owen 8-9-1851
Grisby, W. L. to Leta B. Stewart 8-3-1858
Grisham, Richard to Eliza J. Bowers 9-2-1844 (9-3-1844)
Gross, Francis to Mary Guess 1-20-1848
Gross, George to Sarah Armstrong 8-19-1843 (8-20-1843)
Gross, John to Eliza Jane Bear 2-27-1844 (2-28-1844)
Gross, John to Rachel Collins 5-30-1840 (5-31-1840)
Gross, Masoner to Fisha Gess 12-26-1850
Gross, Pleasant to Polly Dyer 11-12-1845 (11-13-1845)
Grubb, E. to Sarah Martin 9-29-1856
Grubb, Wm. C. to Mary A. Wamac 6-25-1853
Gufey, Jacob to Elisabeth Lowder 6-4-1840
Guine, William to Judy D. Edds 12-30-1847
Guinn, Abner to Malindy Jane Smith 4-11-1850
Gwinn, Geo. W. to Sarah E. Farrar 3-27-1854
Hacker, Julius to Susan Emery 11-15-1844
Hackler, Crisley to Mary Ann Roark 10-6-1840
Hackney, William to Sarah Jones 5-26-1851
Hafley, Cornelius to Malissa J. Ellis 10-16-1854
Hail, Claudius to Delila Ledford 11-26-1843
Hail, George W. to Mary A. Woods 12-18-1845
Hail, M. P. to Sarah Baldwin 8-7-1844
Hair, WM. to Anner Ray 1-27-1840
Hale, George W. to Hetty Padgitt 3-10-1864
Hale, Mark to Nancy Bungrum 12-18-1851
Hall, William to Eleanor Fairbanks 9-22-1847
Haman, Martin to Millie Fitch 8-29-1855
Hambrick, Meigs to Eliza Bunch 10-8-1865
Hamilton, Jesse to Margaret D. Pierce 9-11-1865
Hancock, James M. to Lavina Renow 10-9-1838
Haney, John to Elizabeth Filyan 8-30-1853
Haney, John H. to Adeline Harris 12-9-1864
Hannah, Avery to Matilda Witt 2-1-1842 (1?-3-1842)
Hanner, Avery to Malinda Johnston 4-26-1856
Hany, James to Sarah Ann Rector 5-27-1847
Harden, J. H. to Elizabeth Datters 12-9-1854
Harden, Solomon to Mary Ann Prewitt 6-12-1845
Hardin, Amos to NSancy Bunch 1-18-1841
Hardy, Samuel to Margaret Houpt 10-2-1850

9

Meigs County Grooms

Harred, Allen to Elizabeth Carrell 12-21-1860 (12-23-1860)
Harred, Hiram to Rebecca Smith 2-9-1854
Harris, O. B. to Sarah A.? Peace 6-2-1864
Hart, Lewis to Elizabeth Looney 10-14-1841
Harvison, John to Anjaline Dobbs 3-22-1865
Hatfield, John to Nancy Gray 10-24-1838
Hawey, William to Sarah Dethrage 7-15-1848
Hawser, John M. to Margret Four 12-31-1864
Haynes, John W. to Nancy Miller 5-20-1852
Haynes, Joseph T. to Matilda McCorkle 2-10-1853
Helton, John to Rebecca Goley 6-12-1850
Henly, Edmund to Mary Cahal no dates (with Sep 1840)
Hensley, John to Permely Cooley 7-22-1849
Henson, John to Elizabeth M. Slaughter 8-18-1838 (8-21-1838)
Hewkirk, James H. to Mary Elder 11-27-1842
Hicks, James to Lidian Tolbert 4-27-1858
Hicks, Matthew J. to Nancy Cantrol 11?-1854
Hicks, Richard to Elisabeth Simpson 9-14-1857
Hicks, Thomas J. to Katherine Hatfield 11-22-1845
Higdon, Eleazer L. to Melissa Blevins 1-31-1855
Hinds, James to Eliza Bell 12-24-1854
Hix, Albert to Jane Man 4-19-1845
Hobbs, Jno. to Mary Thornberry 3-30-1839 (4-4-1839)
Hodge, Ambrose W. to Eveline McCorkle 10-6-1847 (10-7-1847)
Hodge, Henry J. to M. Philpot 10-12-1838
Holden, Wm. L. to Mary J. McDaniel 3-20-1865
Holland, Richard to Margaret E. Ackman? 7-25-1857 (7-26-1857)
Holloman, John R. to Mary Baker 3-1-1854
Holman, Burton to Sarah Hutchinson 12-24-1844 (1-3-1845)
Holmes, John R. to Nancy Heaton 1-16-1855
Holt, James H. to Martha J. Wood 7-16-1863
Home, Marion to Ruth Walker 4-13-1864
Homes, Isah to Rachel Sharp 6-12-1846
Hood?, John H. to Mary A. Paul 11-22-1864
Houseley, G. W. to Sarah Elder 5-9-1839
Houser, Ebenezer to Milly Ann Brightwell 6-28-1845 (6-29-1845)
Houser, J. A. to Nancy Miller 1-7-1851
Howard, Abijah to Rachel Bunch 3-16-1862
Howard, John to Elizabeth Atchley 12-18-1852
Howard, M. P. to Sarah Willhelms 7-14-1861 (7-15-1860)
Howell, B. F. to Margt. S. Brown 4-3-1841 (4-4-1841)
Howell, J. A. to Vernein? McCorkle 4-2-1860 (4-10-1860)
Howerton, Jonathan D. to Louiza J. Ledbetter 7-23-1847
Howser, Josiah to Louisa Davis 11-26-1840
Howser, Willet P. to Mahala Mesner 4-13-1865
Hoyle, Jonas to Parthena W. Chatten 9-30-1845 (10-9-1845)
Hoyle, Wm. to Martha Dester 11-6-1838
Huff, B. F. to Nancy Wassen 12-20-1842 (12-22-1842)
Huff, Leonard to Frankey Sears 11-19-1845 (11-20-1845)
Huff, Peter to Suleta Brown 11-25-1841 (12-2-1841)
Hughes, Rice to Martha E. Taff 1-2-1840
Hughs, George to Nancy Riggins 7-2-1858 (7-20-1858)

MEIGS COUNTY, TENNESSEE, MARRIAGES 1851-1865

Meigs County Grooms

Hughs, W. S. to Adda Smith 6-14-1857 (6-16-1857)
Hunter, Anderson to Aslerene Hayslett 11-7-1843 (11-8-1843)
Hunter, Andrew to Angeline McKinley 8-1-1848
Hunter, John to Roena Moore 12-25-1849
Hunter, John P. to Mary T. Johnson 1-5?-1842
Hunter, Robert B. to Craton J. Kincannon 9-25-1854
Hunter, Thomas to Sarah Ann Godsey 11-19-1842 (11-20-1842)
Hunter, William H. to Catharine E. Johnson 6-14-1842 (6-16-1842)
Hutcheson, Cyrus C. to Vilena C. Norman 4-13-1864
Hutcheson, W. L. to Ruth C. Doughty 9-15-1855
Hutchison, Isaac to MSary Stokes 1-29-1840
Hutchison, W. C. to Dorcas A. Hunter 10-20-1850
Hutsell, Elijah to Lucinda Cole 11-1-1841 (11-2-1841)
Hutson, Benjamin to Jane Wan 9-4-1848 (9-5-1848)
Hyde, J. L. to Mary D. Nelson 1-21-1865
Ingle, Adam to Martha Butler 12-14-1865 (1-5-1866)
Ingle, Jacob to Elizabeth J. Malone 12-27-1860
Ingle, Reese to Carline Alford 10-11-1860
Ingle, Wm. to Elizabeth Hunter 10-16-1855
Ingles, John sr. to Barthena Moore 12-21-1843
Isom, Jonathan to Susan Stanley 12-23-1850
Iviline, Thos. to Nancy Marshall 1-1-1851
Jackson, Hesekiah to Sarah Collins 1-4-1860 (1-12-1860)
Jackson, Jas. H. to Mahala Jolley 11-2-1865
Jameson, Milton E. to Mary Vaughn 12-15-1846
Jaquiss, John F. to Mitilda F. Hutdon 10-10-1851
Jaquiss, W. N. to Sarah Deatherage 11-6-1853
Jinkins, J. G. to Maneroy McCorkle 1-24-1851
Jinkins, John to Mary Whaley 9-24-1850
Jinkins, Wm. K. to E. E. Woods 2-24-1842
Johns, Henson T. to Mary Atchley no dates (1850 to 1857)
Johns, Jesse to H. R. Morelan 3-14-1845 (3-17-1845)
Johnson, Ewell to Susan Rowden 12-22-1846 (12-23-1846)
Johnson, Frederick M. to Jane Small 2-10-1846
Johnson, J. G. to Nancy Ann Francisco 11-17-1855
Johnson, James to Hannah Bean 7-8-1844
Johnson, James T. to Mary A. Redmond 12-8-1865 (12-10-1865)
Johnson, Leander M. to Matilda J. Gregory 6-24-1858 (6-25-1858)
Johnson, Madison B. to M. Kinnamond 10-10-1838 (10-12-1838)
Johnson, William to Hariet J. Wadkins 7-1-1844 (7-5-1844)
Johnson, William to Sarah Jane Green 10-18-1848 (10-19-1848)
Jolley, Joseph to Susanna Knight 3-9-1842 (3-11-1842)
Jolly, William to Polly Ward 8-4-1849
Jones, David to Cassander Breedwell 12-25-1843 (12-28-1843)
Jones, Jas. O. to Celia Stokes 7-18-1855
Jones, Milton F. to Nancy Buster 2-4-1843
Jones, Samuel to Dicy Ann Owen 5-22-1846
Jones, Washington to Bethena Faro 10-13-1851
Jones, William to Sarah J. Vetito 11-28-1844
Jordan, Thomas C. to Nancy R. Grigsby 4-11-1844
Keed, John to Mary Philips 12-6-1844 (12-12-1844)
Keller, John to Mahala Cranfell 4-22-1865 (4-23-1865)

11

Meigs County Grooms

Kelley, Mathew to Esther C. Hunter 12-28-1865
Kelly, John to Lorinda Taylor 10-15-1840 (10-18-1840)
Kennedy, Moses to Emily Wilson 11-1-1841 (11-7-1841)
Kerr, John to Nancy Hembree 11-9-1854
Key, William to Catharine McClure 4-18-1849 (4-25-1849)
Keyton, James H. to Sarah Johnson 8-12-1865
Keziah, James to Nancy A. Godsey 5-20-1857
Kincannon, George to Mary J. Barnhart 7-6-1847
Kincannon, Thomas H. to Charlotte J. Miller 6-29-1844
King, Aaron to Martha J. Lillard 4-9-1842
King, Luck? M. to Ruthy E. Ford 12-23-1857
Kinser, Henry to Ellen E. Allen 7-28-1855
Kissur, Dormen to Nelley Correll 9-26-1849
Kitchen, Andrew B. to Susan Tankersley 10-12-1854
Kizer, Jacob to Elizabeth Nelson 7-26-1860
Knight, Abraham to Mahala Blevins 7-20-1844 (7-21-1844)
Knight, Jacob to Nancy Mitchell 4-22-1841
Knight, James H. to Mary E. Gipson 8-30-1865 (9-2-1865)
Knox, Saml. to Susan M. Payne 7-12-1863
Knox, William to Margaret Roork 2-24-1843
Ladd, Enoch to Angelina McCall 3-4-1839 (3-14-1839)
Lane, John M. to Samantha Blevins 3-9-1865
Langford, Wm. to Susan Fine 7-3-1856
Lawson, A. J. to Martha A. Owen 10-4-1865
Lawson, Allen to Dicy (Miss) Lawson 3-24-1838 (3-25-1838)
Lawson, Bartly to Nancy Yonas 1-29-1847
Lawson, Edmond to Margaret Lawson 8-5-1850
Lawson, Isam to Katharine Lawson 7-1-1842
Lawson, John G. to Helena Chambers 4-20-1864
Lawson, Martin to Polly Pettitt 11-22-1844
Lawson, Newton to Mary Ann Armstrong 12-9-1848
Lawson, Thomas J. to Nancy Munsey 9-4-1844
Lawson, Tiry to Charlottie McCorkle 7-18-1848 (8-7-1848)
Lawson, Wm. to Rachel Price 6-8-1854
Lemons, Reuben to Rebecca Daniel 2-28-1855
Leonard, Horatio to Eleanor Collins 7-31-1844 (8-4-1844)
Leonard, T. J. to Sarah Porter 12-21-1850
Leuty, Thos. to Esther P. Eaves 1-10-1839
Lewis, David to Arvicin Crawford 1-4-1840 (1-8-1840)
Lewis, E. to S. C. Calbough 3-24-1860 (3-26-1860)
Lewis, J. W. to Margaret Blevins 12-4-1865 (12-6-1865)
Lewis, Jesse A. to Mary Lock 9-3-1849 (9-5-1849)
Lewis, John H. to Eliner J. Mills 8-21-1851
Lewis, Joshua to Martha Shelton 3-2-1839 (3-3-1839)
Lewis, Thomas to Mary Newman 6-4-1859 (6-5-1859)
Lewman, William to Julian Knight 6-29-1840 (7-5-1840)
Lewy, Thos. H. to L. Tillery 7-14-1839 (7-15-1839)
Lillard, Ashbery S. to Elisha McCorkle 9-30-1849 (10-1-1849)
Lillard, Augustin to Lourinda Kelley 10-10-1850
Lillard, Francis to Loucinda McCorkle 11-19-1853
Lillard, James E. to Sarah Martin 1-19-1860
Lillard, James Sv.? to Mary J. Huff 10-17-1847

Meigs County Grooms

Lillard, John M. to Mary Ann McCartney 6-4-1844
Lillard, John M. to Mertha? Martin 1-1-1860
Lillard, R. M. to Sarah J. McCartney 5-8-1844 (5-9-1844)
Lillard, William M. to Lucretia Thomas 10-22-1845
Lingleton, Green to Mary Branum 6-2-1851
Lock, James H. to Matilda Rogers 6-20-1846
Locke, B. F. to Mary Sharp 11-17-1840 (11-19-1840)
Locke, Josiah to Elizabeth McClellan 9-19-1853
Locke, Linnaeus to Sarah A. Blevins 9-3-1862
Lockmiller, William to Sarah Buster 9-10-1846 (9-13-1846)
Londagan, William to Margaret Mitchell 10-1-1846
Long, Henry to Martha Purdy 7-5-1854
Long, James to Ruth E. Masoner 7-28-1842
Long, Master to Gempy Cox 10-18-1849
Looman, Henry to Jane Bruster 11-31-1846 (12-3-1846)
Losson, Samuel to Sarah Losson 4-10-1843 (4-11-1843)
Lovelace, Jesse jr. to Martha Bishop 12-25-1861
Lovelese, William to Nancy Jane Huff 1-23-1859
Low, Cage to Mary Ann Price 7-3-1845
Low, Robert to Mary E. Small 2-4-1860
Lowery?, Joseph to Mahalyann Coker 5-16-1838
Lucus, Thos.? to Barbara Duke 11-28-1839
Lullman, John H. to Mariah Lumes 7-29-1852
Lunsford, Henry A. to Rebecca Moyers 2-14-1846 (2-19-1846)
Lunsford, Wiley G. to Eliza Myons 2-11-1847
Mabary, Wm. to Drucilla Philips 2-18-1843
Maberry, W. to Elizabeth E. Grigery 5-28-1842 (5-29-1842)
Maden, James to Margaret P. Keywood 1-18-1860 (1-20-1860)
Malone, Wallace to Louisa Moore 11-2-1843
Maner, Stephen to Rebecca Frees? 5-21-1840
Manir, Joseph to Catharine Lason 2-5-1840
Mantooth, Calvin to Vina Harvey 9-7-1844
Mapes, Joseph to Minerva Price 7-29-1846
Maples, W. S. to Elizabeth Elison 9-6-1849
Marshall, Creed F. to Susan Jane Roberds 9-16-1853
Marshall, Ezekiel to Elizabeth Ann Owens 4-6-1844
Marshall, John to Margaret Haney 12-30-1851
Marshall, William to Polly Lewis 10-20-1846
Marshall, William B. to Catharine Blalock 11-16-1854
Martin, Henry to Sarah E. Cox 11-23-1840
Martin, Jesse to Martha McDaniel 6-9-1841
Martin, John to Elisebeth Davis 3-12-1860 (3-13-1860)
Martin, Josiah to Craton Lillard 1-12-1854
Martin, Luke to Nancie Towell 5-29-1851
Martin, Luke P. to Ann Singleton 7-30-1856
Martin, Owen to Sarah Sterns 1-6-1844
Martin, Saml. F. to V. T. Masoner 11-20-1865 (11-22-1865)
Martin, T. J. to Sarah Fox 5-11-1844
Martin, Wilie O. to Eleanor Doughty 11-15-1843 (11-16-1843)
Martin, Wilie O. to Nancy Hutson 1-31-1844
Martin, Wm. to Elizabeth Lockmiller 1-24-1856
Mason, John H. to Rachel Bunch 8-14-1855

13

Meigs County Grooms

Masoner, James M. to Elizabeth Womack 3-6-1861 (3-7-1861)
Massengill, Madison to Elizabeth Knight 8-29-1838 (8-30-18380
Massey, James to Jane Carroll 5-14-1854
Massey, James to Mahaley Forde 9-18-1846
Massey, John to Nancy E. Emry 1-28-1856
Mathews, G. W. to Mary E. Watkins 7-23-1842
Mathis, E. H. to E. A. C. Griffith 3-1-1858
Matlock, Stephen to Polly McClure 7-12-1847
Matthews, Jefferson to Margaret D. Bean 1-13-1844 (1-25-1844)
Matthews, Jesse to Dorcas Mullens 4-8-1842 (4-11-1842)
Maupin, John T. to Hester V. Hutsell 6-10-1864 (6-12-1864)
Mautlon, N. N. to Magdelane Curtan 10-12-1857 (10-13-1857)
Mavity, Andrew J. to Minerva Jane Rigg 1-17-1856
Maynor, Wm. to Mary Moore 12-30-1841
Mays, James to Jane Lewis 7-11-1842 (7-12-1842)
McAdams, James to Mary Neel 7-11-1843
McCable, Archable to Nancey Jane Gibson 10-30-1848 (11-3-1848)
McCain, A. L. to M. A. McCall 7-19-1865 (7-20-1865)
McCall, A. H. to Larena Green 9-4-1841 (9-5-1841)
McCall, Charley to Jane Atchley 1-27-1864 (1-28-1864)
McCall, William to Vina Atchley 1-29-1862 (1-30-1862)
McCallon, James B. to Sarah Jane Butler 9-26-1848 (9-28-1848)
McCallon, John to Emily Dine 12-20-1856
McCallon, Newton H. to Nancy A. Butler 2-18-1856
McCarell, Charles to Eliza Petitt 2-5-1842 (2-6-1842)
McCarrell, Charels to Nancy Corvin 7-26-1843
McCarroll, Wm. jr. to M. Jones 7-13-1839 (7-16-1839)
McCarty, Timothy H. to Mary J. Morison 3-6-1846 (3-10-1846)
McClanahan, H. D. to Elizabeth Lane 10-17-1856
McClanahan, Jno. to P. A. Matthews 5-2-1851
McClanahan, John to Malindar Locke 9-10-1851
McClanahan, Mason to Martha Lock 8-3-1860 (8-5-1860)
McClannahan, Stephen J. to Milia Ramsey 5-2-1844 (5-15-1844)
McClanyhan, John to Sarah Eldridge 8-21-1865
McCollom, Thos. to Sarah Day 9-26-1855
McCollon, A. J. to Sarah Bottom 10-10-1843 (10-12-1843)
McComack, A. W. to Mary E. McClanyhan 7-30-1865
McCorkle, Evander T. to Emaline E. Witt 6-19-1860
McDaniel, John M. to Elinder Quiett 12-4-1850
McDaniel, Saml. to Ann Clark 2-25-1840
McDowell, Daniel to Sarah Simpson 6-16-1838 (6-21-1838)
McDowell, Isaac to Sariah Whitson 2-31-1849 (1-1-1850)
McDowell, James W. to Nancy Baldwin 12-20-1850
McGinnis, Simon to Maryann Gourley 11-8-1838 (12-25-1838)
McInturff, Isaac to Nancy Ann Casey 12-17-1846 (12-22-1846)
McKain, John N.? to Eliza Reace 12-20-1865 (12-25-1865)
McKelpin, John E. to Temperance M. Robeson 6-17-1849 (6-19-1849)
McKenly, W. L. to Barsheba S. Blevins 3-26-1860 (4-1-1860)
McKenzie, Benjamin F. to Marthy M. Jones 9-9-1847
McKenzie, E. G. to Penelope A. Runyon 1-13-1858 (1-16-1858)
McKenzie, G. W. to Susan Kennon? 2-15-1844
McKenzie, Harvey to July Ann Peirce 10-17-1849 (10-18-1849)

Meigs County Grooms

McKenzie, Harvy to Lettitia Brooks 2-3-1841 (2-4-1841)
McKenzie, Jeremiah to Margaret Masoner 12-24-1856
McKenzie, Reuben to Letitia Ann Stewart 6-2-1859
McKeown, Isaac to Matilda Reynolds 11-30-1842 (12-1-1842)
McKinley, John to Manerva Bean 12-15-1849 (12-16-1849)
McKinnie, James to Sarah Snider 12-11-1851
McKnight, Thomas to E. T. Porter 12-24-1861 (12-25-1861)
McMillen, Dillard C. to Hetty Ann Norman 11-4-1841
McMullins, Wm. R. to Barbara Collins 2-22-1842
McNutt, Jas. to Eliz. Sutherland 10-8-1839
McVoy, Henry to Lively Taylor 4-11-1846
Medley, Demascus to Elvina Cox 3-19-1845 (3-21-1845)
Medley, Wm. to Sarah A. George 3-18-1853
Mee, Thomas to Susan Jones 9-2-1855
Melton, J. W. to Anny Crittendon 9-12-1855
Melton, James F. to Jane C. Allen 12-21-1843
Melton, L. M. to Malinda Crow 12-14-1856
Melton, Leander to Marth McMullen 8-15-1847
Melton, William to Mary Ann Correll 10-19-1862
Michael, William D. to Rachel C. Lane 12-2-1844
Michals, A. B. to Nancy Singleton 1-8-1846
Miller, Clayton to Elize Grisby 4-14-1851
Miller, David? to Angeline Elis 12-23-1845
Miller, Henry M. to Sarah M. Peirce 8-15-1849 (8-16-1849)
Miller, Hiram L. to Sarah Martin 1-2-1855
Miller, James to Lucy Brown 8-25-1860
Miller, Jeremiah to Sophia Lewis 9-2-1840 (9-12-1840)
Miller, P. to M. Stuart 11-9-1843
Miller, Pleaseant to Annice Vaughn 1-26-1853
Miller, Thomas to Harret M. Hunter 9-26-1849 (10-4-1849)
Miller, William to Susan Kitten 8-30-1838
Miller, Wright S. to Elizabeth A. Russell 8-12-1847
Millicen, James to Ruth Willes 2-7-1854
Milligan, James to Phebe E. Swaggerty 9-14-1861 (10-15-1861)
Millikin, James to Magana Scott 5-5-1857
Milts, Jos. C. to Sarah Jane Gregory 10-2-1855
Mitchell, David to Katharine Smith 4-6-1846
Mitchell, George to Mary Landagan 11-18-1846
Mitchell, John to Margaret Smith 10-15-1846
Mitchell, John to Nancy Ann Atchley 7-19-1854
Molton, Lilborn to Matilda Melton 2-1-1865
Monger, J. M. to Mary Cantrel 10-7-1857 (10-11-1857)
Monger, Nelson to Mahala E. Redmon 6-13-1856
Mongomery, James to Sarah Cash 2-28-1860
Montgomery, Alex. H. to Martha G. Chattin 7-24-1843
Moody, O. A. to M. V. Moody 7-30-1860 (7-31?-1860)
Moor, James to Susan Dunmore? 8-3-1865 (8-5-1865)
Moore, Alexander to Martha J. Miller 1-20-1851
Moore, David A. to Lucinda Nidiffer 1-11-1840
Moore, Elisha to Ann Mahan 3-27-1860
Moore, Elisha to Minerva Blare 12-27-1847 (1-2-1848)
Moore, F. M. to Martha Reims 10-6-1840

Meigs County Grooms

Moore, Isaac to Telitha Kenedy 6-16-1857 (not executed?)
Moore, J. V.? to Sarah J. Roads 8-3-1857
Moore, James to Mary Day 3-27-1845
Moore, James H. to Sarah A. Francisco 8-15-1841
Moore, John to Matilda C. Brightwell 5-25-1858 (5-27-1858)
Moore, John to Rosana Starns 11-12-1857
Moore, Thomas to Elizabeth Haweson 4-11-1854
Moore, Thomas P. to Sarah H. Wasson 6-22-1861
Moore, Thos. to Nancy Williams 1-23-1841 (4-5-1841)
Moore, William to Eliza Selph 9-12-1848
Moore, William to Polly Farrow 4-29-1843
Moore, Wm. to Nancy Medley 9-22-1853
Moore, Wm. P. to Susan E. Bogeess 7-15-1856
More, Elisha to Milbery Sulivan 10-3-1848 (10-5-1848)
More, James W. to Louisa Jane Geno 10-30-1848
Morgan, James to Betsy Hainy 2-1-1847 (2-2-1847)
Moss, John to Sarah Armitz Rowden 9-29-1853
Moulton, J. N. to Martha J. Curton 8-31-1864
Mouncy, Eli F. to Dilla Fike 11-28-1848 (11-30-1848)
Munsey, Gilbert to Elizabeth Guinn 5-19-1855
Murphey, Philamon to Mary A. Dann(Dean) 9-7-1864
Murphy, John to Mary Jane Pearce 12-11-1864
Murphy, William J. to Sarah A. Lovelace 4-13-1859 (4-14-1859)
Myers, Abner to Elvire More 12-30-1849 (12-31-1849)
Myers, Geoprge to Lewisa Jane Clowse 8-14-1856
Myers, Pleasant to Celia J. Edwards 12-8-1862 (12-10-1862)
Myers, Robert W. to Sopha Starnes 7-20-1853
Myers, W. A. to C. E. Richards 9-15-1857 (9-20-1857)
Myers, William to Lones Reed 12-17-1847 (12-18-1847)
Myers, Wm. to N. J. Parton 9-20-1864
Myers, Wm. R. to Elizabeth C. Cantrell 8-23-1856
Myres, Lesley to Mary Gregory 11-23-1857 (11-24-1857)
Myres, Lesley to Mary Grigary 11-23-1857
Neil, James to Judy Lovisa Reed 8-8-1848 (8-10-1848)
Nelson, Adam to Luise M. Collins 7-8-1859
Nelson, Francis to Frances Canduf 5-12-1851
Nelson, George W. to Mary A. Coffer 11-18-1859
Nelson, Hance to Pheriby Butten 1-7-1847 (not executed)
Nelson, Harison to Joanner Collins 3-19-1851
Newbary, Henry to Sableeche Matthes 10-11-1854
Newcom, David N. to Patience Fore 2-6-1864 (2-7-1864)
Newman, Daniel to Martha Nance 4-1-1851
Newman, John to Bethena Neil 12-5-1857 (12-6-1857)
Newman, Thomas to Elizabeth Shell 4-25-1855
Nite, John to Nancy Nite 4-21-1850
Norman, Claibon? to Angeline Smith 12-29-1862 (not executed)
Norman, Clinton to Catharine Gamble 1-25-1864 (1-26-1864)
Norman, Wm. to Cynthia L. Collins 1-28-1851
Norman, Yance to Elizabeth Buckner 7-27-1843 (7-28-1843)
O'Neal, John J. to Mary Ann Moore 7-23-1844 (7-30-1844)
Okelly, Francis D. to Emilin F. Gerrald 11-14-1839
Orical, Blackburn to Jane Lawson 11-22-1845

Meigs County Grooms

Overton?, Wm. G. to Louisa E. Price 10-5-1841 (10-7-1841)
Owen, Thomas to Brilia Lawson 10-29-1857
Owen, Thos. to Beddy Lawson 10-29-1857
Owens, James M. to Susanna Reynolds 8-14-1849 (8-16-1849)
Owens, John to Rebecca Yonas 1-13-1847
Owens, John to Rebecca Yonas 1-7-1847
Owny, W. J. to Mary M. Witmps 12-25-1852
Pane, Stephen to Mahuldah R. Richards 2-24-1842
Parks, James to Mary Cooley 4-22-1852
Parsons, Emanuel to Rebecca McDowell 11-27-1843
Parsons, Joseph W. to Parthena Crawford 8-12-1843 (8-14-1843)
Paul, B. J. to Adaline Rowden 12-16-1856
Paul, James W. to Mary M. Rowden 11-2-1853
Peak, Newton to Hetty Ann McCallen 11-15-1839 (11-16-1839)
Pearce, Jas. to Mary Day 1-25-1841 (2-4-1841)
Peirce, Thomas B. to Nancy E. Bandy 9-10-1859 (9-11-1859)
Pelfrey, Nathan to Elizabeth Ford 2-9-1841 (2-11-1841)
Penny, Miles P. to Mary Ann Bean 8-26-1848 (8-31-1848)
Peoples, _____ to Vilet Whaly 10-13-1851
Perdy, Joseph to Sarah White 12-13-1851
Perry, Noah to Jane Mavity 9-25-1847
Pervine, Joseph to Annas Rogers 7-28-1860 (7-29-1860)
Pettitt, James to Martha Stout 12-1-1841 (12-2-1841)
Pharis, Doctor to Eliza Ledbetter 2-16-1842 (2-17-1842)
Phariss, Francis M. to Charity Bunch 3-4-1843
Pharriss, William to Elizabeth Goalden 6-18-1840
Philip, James to Margaret Day 10-2-1849 (10-4-1849)
Phillips, Lehu to Elizabeth Fyke 1-7-1840
Pickle, John H. to Sarah S. Winton 8-11-1845 (8-14-1845)
Pierce, Franklin to Sarah Herrid 8-28-1845
Pierce, James F. to Sarah Wamack 3-1-1855
Pierce, James P. to Katharine Day 9-19-1843
Pierce, Philip to Elizabeth Mahan 2-19-1845 (2-20-1845)
Pierce, Thomas D. to Lucy Miller 7-7-1865 (7-22-1865)
Pierce, William F. to Eleanor E. Huie(Hill?) 9-15-1846 (9-16-1846)
Plank, Wm. L. to Mahala Rowden 12-4-1841
Ponston, Henry to Martha M. Bowers 9-19-1839
Poplin, Jehu to Angeline Smith 4-26-1864
Poplin, Wm. to Louisa Bishop 4-15-1854
Poplin, Wm. to Rebecca Cooley 10-9-1864
Powell, John to Mary J. Butler 12-8-1849 (12-9-1849)
Prater, Charles to Mary Holmes 9-15-1838 (9-18-1838)
Prestwood, M. V. to Sarah Lankford 8-1-1857
Preswood, Miles V. to Barbara A. Tillery 2-26-1845 (2-27-1845)
Preswood, Pleasant M. to Elizabeth Tillery 9-24-1844 (9-26-1844)
Prewett, A. J. to Susan Stephens 5-30-1846 (5-31-1846)
Price, Andrew to Nancy Atchley 10-1-1851
Price, Henry to Matilda Horrid 4-15-1851
Price, Henry R. to Hannah J. Irvin 5-27-1862
Price, James to Sarah Areheart 1-13-1861
Price, James T. to Pricey Mapes 1-16-1847
Price, John to Elizabeth Pierce 10-28-1851

Meigs County Grooms

Price, S. P. to Mary Atchley 10-12-1858
Price, Samuel to Catharine McGee 5-30-1853
Price, Samuel to Polly Ann Lankford 5-7-1844 (5-9-1844)
Price, Thomas J. to Mary Mapes 10-19-1846 (10-25-1846)
Price?, John to Rebeccah Rhineheart 6-28-1838 (6-29-1838)
Pugh, Josiah to Highley Auterer 3-1-1859 (3-2-1859)
Purdy, Thomas to Elizabeth C. Melton 8-14-1850
Qualls, George W. to Nancy L. Miller 3-23-1844 (3-24-1844)
Qualls, Nathan jr. to Matilda L. Miller 2-3-1844 (2-5-1844)
Quiett, Cyrus to Nancy Underwood 4-17-1842
Ragan, Z. H. to Lucinda H. Block 8-22-1860 (8-25-1860)
Ramsey, Danl. R. to Lydia T. Day 2-2-1841
Ray, Jacob to Abagail Geiron 10-30-1838
Ray, John to Mary J. Winton 3-2-1849 (3-6-1849)
Ray, Wm. to Rodey McWinton 12-27-1848 (12-29-1848)
Reace, Hugh C. to Eliza Jane Daniel 1?-1855
Rector, Cumberland to Sarah Buster 8-19-1841
Redman, Nelson C. to Elizabeth W. Ragland 10-14-1841
Redman, William to Susan Yeanas 11-26-1857 (11-27-1857)
Redman, Wm. to Betsy West 9-12-1843
Redmon, John P. to Artemiza B. Stockton 1-6-1845
Redmon, Wm. to Mary (Nancy) Robeson 4-4-1838 (4-19-1838)
Renfroe, Joshua to Elizabeth Rowden 4-4-1850
Renfrow, John R. to Susan Rowden 1-3-1851
Renfrow, Robert to Lydia Daniel 12-22-1845
Renfrow, Thomas to Eliza Ford 12-13-1844
Revis, James to Mary Miller 1-16-1850
Revis, James to Mary Stokes 2-25-1854
Reynolds, J. C. to Lewiza Jane Eaves 10-25-1855
Reynolds, William A. to Frances Houser 5-28-1849 (6-1-1849)
Reynolds, William D. to Martha A. E. Vernon 8-6-1849 (8-9-1849)
Reynolds, Wm. A. to Frances Houser 5-28-1840 (1-1-1841?)
Rhea, Richardson to Elizabeth Laves 5-13-1846 (5-14-1846)
Rhea, Thomas to Mary McNutt 8-30-1838 (9-6-1838)
Rhinehart, Emanuel to Polly Ingle 7-17-1844
Rice, Amedia to Emily Taff 10-1-1850
Rice, Calvin to Eliza J. Richardson 11-5-1845 (11-6-1845)
Rice, Richard to Angalina Collins 8-9-1838
Richards, Charles to Pasposia Moss 11-25-1854
Richards, Chas. to Passea Moss 11-25-1853
Richards, Joseph R. to Elizabeth Smith 6-30-1853
Richards, Luke to Emaline F. Greenway 5-22-1854
Richardson, Harvey to Roddy Poplin 12-8-1859
Richardson, James F. to Nancy Moore 12-29-1847
Richardson, John to Martha Stepp 4-27-1857
Richardson, Nathan to Mary J. Rogers 11-27-1845 (11-30-1845)
Richardson, Wm. P. to July Ann Rogers 1-4-1844
Riddle, Eleas to Makalah Brown 12-21-1852
Rigg, W. B. to Scyntha Gannay 6-10-1852
Rigsby, John to Ann Sykes 7-30-1856
Rineheart, William to Elizabeth Poe 11-8-1860
Rineheart, William to Mary Haney 4-13-1858

Meigs County Grooms

Rite, Isaac F. to Martha Bishop 12-29-1860 (12-30-1860)
Rivers, Daniel to Emily J. Wade 12-31-1846
Roark, Harvey to Susan Manerd 3-24-1847
Roark, James to Nancy Holloman 10-6-1851
Roark, John H. to Lutitia Witten 10-18-1847 (10-21-1847)
Roberts, Christopher T. to Malinda J. Runyan 2-2-1864
Robertson, Daniel to Susan M. Bell 10-26-1848 (10-30-1848)
Robeson, Andrew to Elizabeth Black 10-3-1854
Robeson, Calvin C. to Martha L. Guinn 4-29-1850
Robeson, James Madison to Emeretta Fairbanks 9-2-1846 (9-3-1846)
Robeson, John to Malinda Colier 10-19-1851
Robinson, Arthur to Nancy Baker 8-21-1838 (8-26-1838)
Robinson, James to Martha Mabery 8-17-1842
Robinson, James to Mary Breedwell 10-14-1851
Robinson, Thos. T. to Mary J. Hutton 1-30-1865
Rockhold, F. to Susan Lewis 10-2-1865
Rockhold, Wm. to Nancy Melton 3-17-1840
Rogers, Thomas R. to Elizabeth V. McClure 11-12-1845 *
Roishr, John to Elenor McGill 9-19-1851
Romines, Joseph to Adaline Edwards 1-17-1843 (1-18-1843)
Romins, Geo. to Louisa Lawson 12-31-1851
Roods, William to Luisa Voils 2-20-1861
Roork, Thomas to Mary Daniels 8-26-1844 (8-27-1844)
Rothwell, Waller L. to Annis M. Galloway 12-6-1848 (12-7-1848)
Rowden, Elkanah to Jenny Ford 5-23-1851
Rowden, Josie to Mary Ford 1-6-1848
Royl, Wm. to Nancy P. Cox 10-12-1838 (12-21-1838)
Royster, Francis m. to Caroline McGinnis 2-16-1858 (2-18-1858)
Royster, John to Artimissa M. Keeton 11-30-1850
Royster, Joseph G. to Phebe Buttram 5-15-1847
Runyan, Isaac L. to Rivanah M. Blevins 7-25-1860
Russell, David H. to Z. J. Doughty 1-8-1851
Sandusky, Granville C. to Ellen Tennessee Rogers 9-3-1856
Schoolfield, Robert E. to Mary A. Hutcherson 7-5-1849
Scott, John to Nancy Allen 3-18-1854
Scroggins, Wm. C. to Minerva J. Carroll 8-14-1855
Seabourn, Andrew J. to Lucinda Frost 7-18-1849 (7-21-1849)
Sears, Wm. R. to Jane Bennett 1-14-1845 (1-9?-1845)
Seaver, John to Clarissa Gourley 4-11-1846
Sewell, Francis M. to Mary Ann Mavity 10-5-1848
Shahan, John T. to Sarah McCall 12-7-1865
Shamblin, Asel C. to Nancy Stanley 1-9-1853
Shamblin, C. W. to Luisa A. Eldridge 9-6-1860 (9-18-1860)
Sharp, David H. to Mary J. Boggess 7-30-1846 (8-6-1846)
Sharp, Edward to Eliza Shelton 8-16-1842
Sharp, Simon to Jane Pierce 8-23-1857
Sharpe, John to Sarah Ann Boggess 10-21-1849 (10-25-1849)
Shelton, Alexander to Mary Eaton 11-26-1856
Shelton, John to Lydia M. Shelton 4-7-1841 (4-8-1841)
Shelton, Sterling to _____ Gregory 3-10-1840
Shiflet, Francis M. to Permelia Fitchjerls 8-2-1865
Shoat, Elias to Elizabeth Fullington 10-30-1844

Meigs County Grooms

Shoat, Hugh to Nancy Jane Mullins 8-7-1851
Shope, Lewis E. to Eliza J. Tillery 7-25-1865 (7-30-1865)
Simpson, John R. to Sarah Duncy 2-19-1861 (2-21-1861)
Simpson, Robert to Caroline M. Soils 2-12-1861
Simpson, Robert to Eleanor Moyers 4-2-1846
Simpson, Robert to Martha J. Price 8-4-1864 (8-5-1864)
Simson, George M. to Nancy A. Jones 12-15-1852
Singleton, David to Rutha Moyers 11-23-1838 (11-25-1838)
Singleton, William to Mary A. May 12-4-1856
Singleton, Wm. to Nancy Ann May 12-4-1856
Slaughter, Andrew J. to Nancy Lockmiller 9-12-1863 (9-13-1863)
Slaughter, John to Cyntha Ann Howard 6-15-1858? (6-16-1858?)
Slauter?, Jacob to Kisiah Guinn 1-13-1858 (1-14-1858)
Sligar, Henry to Lydia Simpson 11-22-1846
Sligar, James to Sarah Sligar 10-1-1864 (10-2-1864)
Sliger, Jackson to Kiziah Payne 1-5-1858
Sluter, John to Rebecca Swofford 2-29-1842
Small, Henry to Hannah Wan 4-9-1846
Small, John to Sarah Wan 9-24-1845 (9-25-1845)
Smith, A. B.? to Mary Jane Warrick 9-18-1844
Smith, Aaron to Lucinda Walden 1-29-1839 (1-30-1839)
Smith, Charles to Mahala Rice 7-20-1858
Smith, Elijah S. to Mary J. Winton 4-4-1844
Smith, G. T. to Loucinda Heney 1-17-1860 (1-18-1860)
Smith, Jackson to Elizabeth Ann Price 7-6-1862
Smith, James to Sarah Guinn 4-11-1850
Smith, John to Frances Snow 9-22-1838 (10-2-1838)
Smith, John W. to Pheaby Moore 9-15-1838 (10-5-1838)
Smith, John W. to Sarah Little 2-10-1842
Smith, Jordan to Polly Snow 1-12-1842
Smith, Joshua L. to Marietta Hunter 10-26-1865
Smith, R. to Margaret Bondwell 6-18-1844 (6-20-1844)
Smith, William to Rebecca Hill 12-14-1843
Smith, Wilson C. to Eleanor Blevins 3-10-1841 (6-1-1849?)
Smith, Wm. A. to Dicy Sears 11-24-1845 (11-26-1845)
Smith, Wm. E. to Jailey L. Woods 5-2-1861 (5-2-1861)
Smith, Wm. J. to Nancy C. Cranfill 9-15-1864
Smith, Wright to Jane Sharp 11-29-1843 (11-30-1843)
Snider, A. R. to Mahala Rogers 10-22-1850
Snow, Samuel to Elizabeth Maberry 12-28-1843
Sparks, Israel to Marthy Curvis 1?-1855
Sparks, Thomas to Mary Philpott 5-31-1843
Spicer, Henry L. to Mirian King 1-5-1856
Spicer, William J. to Susan J. King 8-11-1853
Standfield, John to Susas Duning 4-5-1851
Stanley, John L. to Nancy Ann Johns 8-25-1854
Stanner, Thomas E. to Elizabeth A. Edds 9-19-1849
Stapleton, Thos. to Anna Lawson 5-15-1841
Starnes, John to Elizabeth Chapman 12-6-1844
Starnes, Joshua to Cylva Jane Johns 7-26-1851
Starns, B. F. to Louisa Pellason 10-14-1851
Steen, James M. to Sarah Ford 8-10-1846 (8-13-1846)

Meigs County Grooms

Stephens, Martin H. to Eda Caroline Simpson 4-13-1848
Stewart, Joseph to Ann King 9-11-1839 (9-12-1839)
Stewart, Levi F. to Louisa Neil 9-4-1860
Stewart, Matthew B. to Mary C. Lentz? 4-26-1864 4-29?-1864)
Stewart, Wm. to Texas Lillard 2-23-1861
Stockton, Daniel G. to Miry McDaniel 1-11-1855
Stockton, H. P. to Elizabeth Crew 7-25-1850
Stockton, Samuel to Sarah Earnestine Stockton 5-29-1850
Stockton, Thos. P. to M. E. Boggiss 6-15-1839
Stokes, James to Martha A. Lawson 12-9-1852
Stokes, Thomas C. to Mary Perry 1-15-1846
Stokes, William to Matilda Coxey 11-13-1845 *
Stone, James to Elizabeth Welchhance 3-18-1851
Storris, Henry to Narcis Johns 1-11-1861 (1-13-1861)
Stuart, Andrew to Lurenna Inman 2-18-1843 (2-19-1843)
Stuart, Joseph to Huldah Jones 2-10-1842 (2-11-1842)
Swafford, James to Mary C. Curton 9-10-1856
Swagerty?, J. T. to Mary M. Dolen 12-29-1865
Sweatman, A. to Sarah Price 8-10-1847
Taff, A. G. to S. A. Patterson 12-19-1857 (12-20-1857)
Taff, Calvin R. to Nancy Collins 9-27-1847 (9-30-1847)
Taff, John jr. to Nancy Ann Melton 7-25-1858
Talley?, A. B. to Abegail Baker 1-16-1860
Tankersley, Saml. G. to Malinda Moore 6-13-1863
Tankesley, Richard to Mary Coffer 4-18-1857 (4-19-1857)
Taylor, James to Vilety Slinger 12-14-1850
Taylor, Jeremiah to Mary Munsey 8-14-1863
Taylor, John B. to Ann Cross 2-23-1858 (2-25-1858)
Taylor, Richard to Mary Stewart 12-11-1851
Tharp, Robert to Louisa Selvage 8-15-1865
Tharpe, Alexander to Dicey Ann Jones 2-24-1849 (2-25-1849)
Thomas, B. F. to Evaline T. Price 1-29-1865 (1-30-1865)
Thomas, James to Mary J. Neil 2-15-1853
Thompson, Elisha D. to Nancy L. McEwin 3-7-1853
Thornberry, Peter to Mary Cady 7-20-1839 (7-23-1839)
Thorp, Wm. to Ann Rhinheart 9-20-1841 (1-1-1849?)
Thurman, James to Susan Brazill 10-25-1854
Tillery, Coffield to Eliza J. Garrow 9-30-1851
Tillery, Coffield to Nancy Fuller 7-14-1839
Tillery, Huey to Elizabeth Cate 2-25-1858
Tillery, Hugh to Belinda Broks 2-5-1840
Tillery, Jacob to Louisa Price 7-31-1845
Tillery, John to Nancy Rogers 2-1-1845
Tillerz, Wm. to Margaret J. Achly 12-28-1865 (1-27-1866)
Tilly, Thomas P. to Nancy R. Houser 2-4-1860 (2-5-1860)
Tims, Washington to Mary O'Neal 8-19-1848 (8-20-1848)
Tindel, Jno. to _____ Wilhelms 9-1-1839 (9-12-1839)
Trusler, Delaney to Elizabeth Sulivan 2-25-1846 (2-26-1846)
Tuell, John R. to Nancy Lovisa Owen 9-6-1855
Turner, Robert to Abbigail Williams 11-12-1861 (11-20-1861)
Vandergrift, Andre to Nancy Bedsoles 7-31-1854
Vanzart, Henry C. to Nancy McKown 2-28-1848 (2-29-1848)

Meigs County Grooms

Vaughan, John to Sarah Melton 2-26-1840 (4-18-1840)
Vaughn, Aron to Emaline White 5-6-1860
Vaughn, Murphree H. to Mahala Webb 10-31-1849 (11-1-1849)
Vaughn, Nathan A. to Catharine Adams 10-14-1858
Vincent, Euel to Sarah Atckinson 1-15-1861
Vincent, Samuel to Liza Jane Miller 2-7-1854
Vincent, Wm. J. to Evaline Miller 1-12-1854
Walker, Creed to Martha Rivers 7-6-1840 (7-7-1840)
Walker, David to Nancy Edgemon 12-20-1841 (12-23-1841)
Walker, Jno. to Rachel Cox 6-5-1839 (6-6-1839)
Walker, S. J. to ? ? 1853
Walker, Thomas to Martha Ann Carvin? 4-1-1865 (4-2-1865)
Waller, A. L. to Mary Duckworth 8-21-1865 (8-22-1865)
Wallin, Samuel to Delpha Keelin 6-27-1859 (9-3-1839)
Walling, John to C. Butram 6-27-1840
Wamac, Daniel to Sarah Ann Cate 9-8-1855
Wamack, Daniel to Julia Grubb 2-10-1859 (2-13-1859)
Wamack, Samuel M. to Mary J. Norman 10-6-1862 (10-5?-1862)
Wan, Daniel to Sarah J. Hague 5-13-1839 (6-6-1839)
Wan, Wm. to Elizabeth Gibson 1-23-1845 (4-7-1845)
Ward, Henry P. to Celia Jane Stockton 9-9-1853
Ward, James H. to Irena Gerl 4-14-1842 (6-7-1842)
Ward, Nicodemus to Nancy Isley 5-29-1843 (7-12-1843)
Ward, Wm. L. to Martha Smith 9-12-1864
Warmack, sJohn to Dolly Loony 11-7-1840 (1-1-1841)
Wassum, A. S. to Ruth J. Moore 2-20-1860 (2-23-1860)
Waterhouse, Darius to Harriet C. Sharp 5-4-1846 (5-7-1846)
Watkins, John to Sarah Walker 9-20-1855
Watson, Nathaniel to Sarah McRennels 9-28-1847
Watson, W. C. to Emly Jane Stephens 9-28-1852
Watson, William to Sariah Mapes 8-9-1849
Watts, Wm. to Rachel Lawson 7-20-1855
Wear, L. L. to M. M. Hounshell 7-19-1840
Webb, B. F. to A. E. Housley 9-5-1865
Webb, Jacob to Sarah E. Phillips 8-16-1864 (8-18-1864)
Webb, John W. to Mary? A. Lockman 10-3-1865
Weir, Robert L. to Amanda A. Hickey 9-11-1851
Weitt?, William C. to Margret Owens 10-20-1860 (10-21-1860)
Welch, C. M. K.(Charles) to Sarah Ann McClaren 12-25-1841 (12-26-18
West, E. J. to Carline Larrants 5-5-1860 (5-6-1860)
West, Jackson to Dicy Roork 3-21-1843
West, Wm. to Mary Coggins 8-12-1865
White, John T. to Parry Miller 7-10-1851
White, M. A. to Mary Rice 9-2-1851
White, Maidson to Julia Ann Malone 9-17-1853
Whiteside, William to Myra Campbell 2-19-1851
Whitmore, H. to Martha Rigg 2-9-1860
Whitsides, James to Martha Cooley 5-21-1857
Widows, Isaac to Barbary Keneda 12-26-1850
Wier, Elias L. to S. P. Mathis 11-22-1838 (11-23-1838)
Wilhelms, James to Abigail Atchley 1-25-1843
William, Shadrack to Nancy M. King 10-18-1850

Meigs County Grooms

Williams, Charles to Katharine Buckner 3-2-1843
Williams, Greene to Elizabeth Whitmore 11-10-1862 (11-12-1862)
Williams, Henry to Charity Jones 11-11-1864
Williams, Hosea H. to Sarah Farmer 4-19-1838 (5-24-1838)
Williams, Jacob to Mary Johnson 11-12-1861 (11-14-1861)
Williams, John to Frances Ann Fowler 11-12-1861 (10-13-1861)
Williams, John W. to Louisa Whitmore 12-23-1852
Williams, Rhuben J. to Elizabeth Lawson 10-8-1857
Williams, Tinsley to Mary Forrest 9-19-1851
Wills, David to Elizabeth Iseley 3-7-1843
Wilson, George . to Elizabeth Woods 6-11-1842 (6-14-1842)
Wilson, Wm. H. to Elizabeth Tankersley 6-8-1861 (8-5-1861)
Wirick, Frederick to Sarah Rogers 10-5-1841
Wit, Joseph N. to Charity A. Gamble 8-18-1849 (8-23-1849)
Witt, James to Catherine Gross 9-16-1856
Witt, Jesse to Harriet E. Shiply 7-28-1860 (7-29-1860)
Witt, Jos. H. to Mary I. Whitmore 10-29-1856
Witt, Nat? to Jennetta Wood 3-1-1860 (3-2-1860)
Witt, Wm. A. to Elizabeth Royster 7-30-1842 (7-31-1842)
Witten, Joshua E. to Nancy Roark 11-26-1846 (11-30-1846)
Wood, John to Telitha McAdams 10-1-1839 (10-3-1839)
Wood, Jonathan to Louisa E. Broweder 11-16-1850
Wood, Jonathan to NSancy A. Hounshell 5-23-1844
Wood, W. L. to Louisa J. Price 11-14-1864
Woods, S. W. to Nancy E. Brown 1-28-1841
Woody, Samuel to Elizabeth Rew 4-3-1850
Wright, James W. to Parthena Armstrong 9-13-1865 (9-29-1865)
Wright, William to Sarah K. Howard 7-26-1862 (7-27-1862)
Young, Carter to Peggy Grissum 9-26-1838 (9-27-1838)
Young, John to Eliza Emeline Helton 12-7-1847 (12-9-1847)
Young, Thomas to Margrett Mariah Correll 10-20-1849 (10-21-1849)
Young, W. J. to Larky Elkin 8-31-1850
Zeigler, Jacob to Tennepe Miller 10-21-1851

Marriages Arranged Alphabetically

By

BRIDE

Meigs County Brides

?, ? to S. J. Walker 1853
Achly, Margaret J. to Wm. Tillerz 12-28-1865 (1-27-1866)
Ackman?, Margaret E. to Richard Holland 7-25-1857 (7-26-1857)
Adams, Catharine to Nathan A. Vaughn 10-14-1858
Adams, Elizabeth to Philip M. Dake 10-13-1853
Adams, Mary to T. A. Davis 9-6-1865
Adams, Polly to John Davis 12-19-1840
Alford, Carline to Reese Ingle 10-11-1860
Alford, Sarah Jan to Gideon Branham 10-6-1859
Alfred, Lemsea to James Beady 9-9-1852
Allen, Ellen E. to Henry Kinser 7-28-1855
Allen, Jane C. to James F. Melton 12-21-1843
Allen, Nancy to John Scott 3-18-1854
Arehart, Mary S. to John E. Griffith 8-4-1856
Areheart, Sarah to James Price 1-13-1861
Armstrong, Attanzana to John Fox 1-28-1851
Armstrong, Eliza to Elgin Brightwell 8-19-1843 (8-20-1843)
Armstrong, Elizabeth J. to William A. Cuningham 8-5-1858
Armstrong, Mahaley to Jefferson Brightwell 3-21-1858 (3-23-1858)
Armstrong, Mary Ann to Newton Lawson 12-9-1848
Armstrong, Parthena to James W. Wright 9-13-1865 (9-29-1865)
Armstrong, Polina to Wm. W. Blankenship 11-11-1857
Armstrong, Sarah to George Gross 8-19-1843 (8-20-1843)
Atchley, Abigail to James Wilhelms 1-25-1843
Atchley, Elizabeth to John Howard 12-18-1852
Atchley, Jane to Charley McCall 1-27-1864 (1-28-1864)
Atchley, Lucy Ann to Jno. S. Ackman? 9-17-1863
Atchley, Mary to Henson T. Johns no dates (1850 to 1857)
Atchley, Mary to S. P. Price 10-12-1858
Atchley, Nancy to Andrew Price 10-1-1851
Atchley, Nancy Ann to John Mitchell 7-19-1854
Atchley, Vina to William McCall 1-29-1862 (1-30-1862)
Atckinson, Sarah to Euel Vincent 1-15-1861
Atkinson, Elizabeth A. to Pleasant H. Davis 3-20-1856
Atkinson, Emily to James Carter 9-1-1843
Auterer, Highley to Josiah Pugh 3-1-1859 (3-2-1859)
Bagwell, Nancy F. to George Foosher 5-22-1857 (5-25-1857)
Baker, Abegail to A. B. Talley? 1-16-1860
Baker, Elisabeth to Champanius Baker 9-30-1847
Baker, Harriet to Isaac Curtin 2-7-1854
Baker, Mary to John R. Holloman 3-1-1854
Baker, Nancy to Arthur Robinson 8-21-1838 (8-26-1838)
Baker, Sarah to Alford Gibson 3-11-1842 (3-13-1842)
Baldwin, Nancy to James W. McDowell 12-20-1850
Baldwin, Sarah to M. P. Hail 8-7-1844
Bandy, Nancy E. to Thomas B. Peirce 9-10-1859 (9-11-1859)
Barmon, N. J. to Rufus Furguson 11-19-1849 (11-20-1849)
Barnett, Martha J. to Wm. Blankenship 9-15-1853
Barnett, Sarah to M. Fooshee 1-22-1859 (1-27-1859)

27

Meigs County Brides

Barnhart, Mary J. to George Kincannon 7-6-1847
Bayless, Marthey to William Blythe 11-12-1849
Bean, Hannah to James Johnson 7-8-1844
Bean, Manerva to John McKinley 12-15-1849 (12-16-1849)
Bean, Margaret D. to Jefferson Matthews 1-13-1844 (1-25-1844)
Bean, Mary Ann to Miles P. Penny 8-26-1848 (8-31-1848)
Bear, Eliza Jane to John Gross 2-27-1844 (2-28-1844)
Bedsoles, Nancy to Andre Vandergrift 7-31-1854
Bell, Eliza to James Hinds 12-24-1854
Bell, Sarah to Wm. T. Armstrong 3-29-1842
Bell, Susan M. to Daniel Robertson 10-26-1848 (10-30-1848)
Bennet, Martha to Wallas Blankenship 11-6-1860
Bennett, Elizabeth to William Davis 9-10-1845
Bennett, Jane to Wm. R. Sears 1-14-1845 (1-9?-1845)
Benson, Sarah F. to John L. Ellis 7-11-1850
Benton, Eliza to Samuel A. Cate 3-26-1865
Bishop, Louisa to Wm. Poplin 4-15-1854
Bishop, Martha to Jesse jr. Lovelace 12-25-1861
Bishop, Martha to Isaac F. Rite 12-29-1860 (12-30-1860)
Bishop, Mary to Louis Benton 12-5-1857
Black, Elizabeth to Andrew Robeson 10-3-1854
Blackwell, Emily to Joseph Blackwell 2-27-1865
Blackwell, Emily to Jefferson Crabtree 11-1-1862
Blackwell, Minerva to Jessey Bell 2-22-1854
Blakely, Harriet to Philip Blevens 12-6-1838
Blalock, Catharine to William B. Marshall 11-16-1854
Blankenship, Delpha to William Allen 7-13-1841
Blankenship, Pernado to James Cunningham 2-14-1855
Blankenship, Sarah to Wm. Eaves 7-12-1855
Blare, Minerva to Elisha Moore 12-27-1847 (1-2-1848)
Blaylock, Lucy to Samuel Foster 7-20-1852
Blaylock, M. A. to S. H. Blaylock 10-25-1857
Blaylock, Sarah A. to E. P. Blaylock 1-28-1865
Bledsoe, Elizabeth to Pleasant Gallaher 8-9-1863
Blevins, Amanda E. to Res. Blevins 5-25-1851
Blevins, Barsheba S. to W. L. McKenly 3-26-1860 (4-1-1860)
Blevins, Catharine to Wm. Collins 1-16-1851
Blevins, D. E. to F. G. Adams 6-15-1863 (6-16-1863)
Blevins, Eleanor to Wilson C. Smith 3-10-1841 (6-1-1849?)
Blevins, Lisa to John Gourley 11-19-1857
Blevins, Mahala to Abraham Knight 7-20-1844 (7-21-1844)
Blevins, Margaret to J. W. Lewis 12-4-1865 (12-6-1865)
Blevins, Melissa to Eleazer L. Higdon 1-31-1855
Blevins, Nancy to Harrison Blevins 11-23-1848
Blevins, Rivanah M. to Isaac L. Runyan 7-25-1860
Blevins, Samantha to John M. Lane 3-9-1865
Blevins, Sarah A. to Linnaeus Locke 9-3-1862
Blevins, Sarah Jane to Jno. D. Gourly 1-6-1859
Block, Lucinda H. to Z. H. Ragan 8-22-1860 (8-25-1860)
Blyth, Rebeca to David Fullington 5-3-1851

Meigs County Brides

Bogeess, Susan E. to Wm. P. Moore 7-15-1856
Boggess, Hariet C. to Robert R. Davis 10-31-1843 (11-2-1843)
Boggess, Mary J. to David H. Sharp 7-30-1846 (8-6-1846)
Boggess, Sarah Ann to John Sharpe 10-21-1849 (10-25-1849)
Boggiss, M. E. to Thos. P. Stockton 6-15-1839
Bondwell, Margaret to R. Smith 6-18-1844 (6-20-1844)
Bottom, Sarah to A. J. McCollon 10-10-1843 (10-12-1843)
Bottoms, Caroline C. to J. R. Douglass 12-9-1847
Bower, Kitha to L. B. Cox 10-23-1843 (10-24-1843)
Bowers, Eliza J. to Richard Grisham 9-2-1844 (9-3-1844)
Bowers, Martha M. to Henry Ponston 9-19-1839
Branum, Mary to Green Lingleton 6-2-1851
Braziel, Mary to Larcum Braziel 2-9-1854
Brazill, Susan to James Thurman 10-25-1854
Breedwell, Cassander to David Jones 12-25-1843 (12-28-1843)
Breedwell, Mary to James Robinson 10-14-1851
Brightwell, Matilda C. to John Moore 5-25-1858 (5-27-1858)
Brightwell, Milly Ann to Ebenezer Houser 6-28-1845 (6-29-1845)
Brighwell, Leter to Paul Bunch 2-3-1851
Brogdon, Jane to George Colbaugh 3-9-1865
Broks, Belinda to Hugh Tillery 2-5-1840
Brooks, Juda Ann to Noah Atchley 10-25-1865 (1-5-1866)
Brooks, Lettitia to Harvy McKenzie 2-3-1841 (2-4-1841)
Broweder, Louisa E. to Jonathan Wood 11-16-1850
Brown, Lucy to James Miller 8-25-1860
Brown, Makalah to Eleas Riddle 12-21-1852
Brown, Margt. S. to B. F. Howell 4-3-1841 (4-4-1841)
Brown, Martha to Leander Faris 7-13-1850
Brown, Nancy E. to S. W. Woods 1-28-1841
Brown, Suleta to Peter Huff 11-25-1841 (12-2-1841)
Bruster, Jane to Henry Looman 11-31-1846 (12-3-1846)
Buckler, Alsia to John Alison 11-7-1847
Buckner, Elizabeth to Yance Norman 7-27-1843 (7-28-1843)
Buckner, Katharine to Charles Williams 3-2-1843
Bunch, Charity to Francis M. Phariss 3-4-1843
Bunch, Eliza to Meigs Hambrick 10-8-1865
Bunch, Mariah to Troy F. Collins 4-17-1855
Bunch, Mary to Martin Farless 11-30-1843
Bunch, NSancy to Amos Hardin 1-18-1841
Bunch, Rachel to Abijah Howard 3-16-1862
Bunch, Rachel to John H. Mason 8-14-1855
Bungrum, Nancy to Mark Hale 12-18-1851
Burcham, Sophia A. to John Cole 6-18-1844 (6-20-1844)
Burton, Lydia to William J. Gray 5-23-1838 (7-2-1838)
Buster, Jane to Joseph A. Atchly 9-16-1860
Buster, L. to Charles Franklin 8-17-1839 (9-3-1839)
Buster, Nancy to Milton F. Jones 2-4-1843
Buster, Sarah to William Lockmiller 9-10-1846 (9-13-1846)
Buster, Sarah to Cumberland Rector 8-19-1841
Butler, Agnes to Wm. B. Ford 3-10-1841

Meigs County Brides

Butler, Eliza to Geo. Fullington 8-7-1893
Butler, Martha to Adam Ingle 12-14-1865 (1-5-1866)
Butler, Mary J. to John Powell 12-8-1849 (12-9-1849)
Butler, Nancy A. to Newton H. McCallon 2-18-1856
Butler, Sarah Jane to James B. McCallon 9-26-1848 (9-28-1848)
Butram, C. to John Walling 6-27-1840
Butten, Pheriby to Hance Nelson 1-7-1847 (not executed)
Buttram, Phebe to Joseph G. Royster 5-15-1847
Cady, Mary to Peter Thornberry 7-20-1839 (7-23-1839)
Cahal, Mary to Edmund Henly no dates (with Sep 1840)
Calbough, S. C. to E. Lewis 3-24-1860 (3-26-1860)
Campbell, Myra to William Whiteside 2-19-1851
Canduf, Frances to Francis Nelson 5-12-1851
Cantrel, Mary to J. M. Monger 10-7-1857 (10-11-1857)
Cantrell, Elizabeth C. to Wm. R. Myers 8-23-1856
Cantrol, Nancy to Matthew J. Hicks 11?-1854
Caps, Harriete to James Adams 1-20-1849 (1-21-1849)
Caril, Delisa to Samuel H. Gourley 7-16-1844
Carrell, Elizabeth to Allen Harred 12-21-1860 (12-23-1860)
Carrell, Ruthy to Benjamon Bunch 6-19-1858 (6-26-1858)
Carroll, Jane to James Massey 5-14-1854
Carroll, Minerva J. to Wm. C. Scroggins 8-14-1855
Carvin?, Martha Ann to Thomas Walker 4-1-1865 (4-2-1865)
Casey, Elizabeth M. to Adam Davis 2-23-1853
Casey, Mary C. to Thomas E. Crossland 7-4-1846 (7-9-1846)
Casey, Nancy Ann to Isaac McInturff 12-17-1846 (12-22-1846)
Cash, Sarah to James Mongomery 2-28-1860
Cate, Elizabeth to Huey Tillery 2-25-1858
Cate, Sarah Ann to Daniel Wamac 9-8-1855
Chambers, Helena to John G. Lawson 4-20-1864
Chapman, Elizabeth to John Starnes 12-6-1844
Chatten, Parthena W. to Jonas Hoyle 9-30-1845 (10-9-1845)
Chattin, Martha G. to Alex. H. Montgomery 7-24-1843
Childress, Louisa E. to James Browden 12-19-1843
Clanahan, Catharine to John Cooley 10-14-1851
Clark, Ann to Saml. McDaniel 2-25-1840
Clark, Glopha to Thomas Edgemon 7-21-1842
Clingan, Mary to John J. Dean 7-1-1864 (7-3-1864)
Clowse, Lewisa Jane to Geoprge Myers 8-14-1856
Cofer, Nancy Ann to William J. Boll 8-30-1860 (9-2-1860)
Coffer, Mary to Richard Tankesley 4-18-1857 (4-19-1857)
Coffer, Mary A. to George W. Nelson 11-18-1859
Coffey, Sarah to Daniel W. Chambers 10-14-1843
Coggins, Mary to Wm. West 8-12-1865
Coker, Mahalyann to Joseph Lowery? 5-16-1838
Cole, Lucinda to Elijah Hutsell 11-1-1841 (11-2-1841)
Colier, Malinda to John Robeson 10-19-1851
Collins, Angalina to Richard Rice 8-9-1838
Collins, Barbara to Wm. R. McMullins 2-22-1842
Collins, Cynthia L. to Wm. Norman 1-28-1851

Meigs County Brides

Collins, Eleanor to Horatio Leonard 7-31-1844 (8-4-1844)
Collins, Jane to James A. Cowan 7-24-1844 (7-25-1844)
Collins, Joanner to Harison Nelson 3-19-1851
Collins, Lucresia to Jesse Baker 9-14-1853
Collins, Luise M. to Adam Nelson 7-8-1859
Collins, Margaret to Abraham I. Godsey 2-1-1851
Collins, Nancy to Calvin R. Taff 9-27-1847 (9-30-1847)
Collins, Rachel to John Gross 5-30-1840 (5-31-1840)
Collins, Sarah to Hesekiah Jackson 1-4-1860 (1-12-1860)
Colvin, Margret to Jesse W. Dobbs 8-30-1845 (9-3-1845)
Cooke, Melvina to N. Drake 5-31-1863 (6-14-1863)
Cooley, Martha to James Whitsides 5-21-1857
Cooley, Mary to James Parks 4-22-1852
Cooley, Permely to John Hensley 7-22-1849
Cooley, Rebecca to Wm. Poplin 10-9-1864
Coop, Artemiza to William Arrants 2-13-1845
Correll, Margrett Mariah to Thomas Young 10-20-1849 (10-21-1849)
Correll, Mary Ann to William Melton 10-19-1862
Correll, Mary Isley James to Barba Towsa Bumham 1-30-1851
Correll, Nelley to Dormen Kissur 9-26-1849
Corvin, Adaline to William Corvin 6-14-1865
Corvin, Nancy to Charels McCarrell 7-26-1843
Cox, Elvina to Demascus Medley 3-19-1845 (3-21-1845)
Cox, Emaline to Ishmael A. Godsey 6-15-1847
Cox, Gempy to Master Long 10-18-1849
Cox, Harriet to Reece B. Cross 2-10-1850
Cox, Matilda to Andrew Cox 7-26-1865 (7-27-1865)
Cox, Nancy J. to Edwin D. Gilbert 12-19-1854
Cox, Nancy P. to Wm. Royl 10-12-1838 (12-21-1838)
Cox, Rachel to Jno. Walker 6-5-1839 (6-6-1839)
Cox, Sarah Ann to Edward F. Cox 8-16-1851
Cox, Sarah E. to Henry Martin 11-23-1840
Coxey, Matilda to William Stokes 11-13-1845 *
Craighead, M. J. to A. W. Frazier 9-1-1858 (9-2-1858)
Cranfell, Mahala to John Keller 4-22-1865 (4-23-1865)
Cranfill, Nancy C. to Wm. J. Smith 9-15-1864
Crawford, Arvicin to David Lewis 1-4-1840 (1-8-1840)
Crawford, Parthena to Joseph W. Parsons 8-12-1843 (8-14-1843)
Crew, Elizabeth to H. P. Stockton 7-25-1850
Crittendon, Anny to J. W. Melton 9-12-1855
Cross, Ann to John B. Taylor 2-23-1858 (2-25-1858)
Crow, Malinda to L. M. Melton 12-14-1856
Crow, Matilda to W. O. Allen 4-29-1856
Curtain, Magdaline to Newton Bowers 9-12-1861 (9-15-1861)
Curtain?, Narcissus to Thomas Gregory 11-30-1861 (12-3-1861)
Curtan, Magdelane to N. N. Mautlon 10-12-1857 (10-13-1857)
Curton, Martha J. to J. N. Moulton 8-31-1864
Curton, Mary C. to James Swafford 9-10-1856
Curvis, Marthy to Israel Sparks 1?-1855
Daniel, Acilla A. to Jas. Griffin 3-17-1840

Meigs County Brides

Daniel, Eliza Jane to Hugh C. Reace 1?-1855
Daniel, Lydia to Robert Renfrow 12-22-1845
Daniel, Rebecca to Reuben Lemons 2-28-1855
Daniels, Mary to Thomas Roork 8-26-1844 (8-27-1844)
Dann(Dean), Mary A. to Philamon Murphey 9-7-1864
Datters, Elizabeth to J. H. Harden 12-9-1854
Davis, Elisebeth to John Martin 3-12-1860 (3-13-1860)
Davis, Isabella to Franklin Brogden 6-24-1856
Davis, Louisa to Josiah Howser 11-26-1840
Davis, Pheba to John Gardner 6-17-1849
Davis, Rebecca to Wm. Brison 8-31-1856
Davis, Sarah to Wiley B. Clack 11-28-1852
Day, Katharine to James P. Pierce 9-19-1843
Day, Lydia T. to Danl. R. Ramsey 2-2-1841
Day, Margaret to James Philip 10-2-1849 (10-4-1849)
Day, Mary to James Moore 3-27-1845
Day, Mary to Jas. Pearce 1-25-1841 (2-4-1841)
Day, Sarah to Thos. McCollom 9-26-1855
Dearman, Matilda J. to Thomas J. Eaves 12-18-1841 (12-19-1841)
Deatherage, Sarah to W. N. Jaquiss 11-6-1853
Denton, Mary A. to J. F. Elder 8-2-1858 (8-3-1858)
Dester, Martha to Wm. Hoyle 11-6-1838
Dethrage, Sarah to William Hawey 7-15-1848
Dien, Charity to John Durham 9-6-1851
Dine, Emily to John McCallon 12-20-1856
Dixon?, Eliza to William Blackwell 3-29-1838
Dobbs, Anjaline to John Harvison 3-22-1865
Dolen, Mary M. to J. T. Swagerty? 12-29-1865
Doughty, Eleanor to Wilie O. Martin 11-15-1843 (11-16-1843)
Doughty, Ruth C. to W. L. Hutcheson 9-15-1855
Doughty, Z. J. to David H. Russell 1-8-1851
Duckworth, Mary to A. L. Waller 8-21-1865 (8-22-1865)
Duke, Barbara to Thos.? Lucus 11-28-1839
Duncy, Sarah to John R. Simpson 2-19-1861 (2-21-1861)
Duning, Susas to John Standfield 4-5-1851
Dunmore?, Susan to James Moor 8-3-1865 (8-5-1865)
Dyer, Polly to Pleasant Gross 11-12-1845 (11-13-1845)
Eakin, Caty to Hugh Baker 5-21-1840 (6-18-1840)
Eaton, Mary to Alexander Shelton 11-26-1856
Eaves, Esther P. to Thos. Leuty 1-10-1839
Eaves, Lewiza Jane to J. C. Reynolds 10-25-1855
Edds, Elizabeth A. to Thomas E. Stanner 9-19-1849
Edds, Judy D. to William Guine 12-30-1847
Edgemon, Lousanna to John A. Clark 11-22-1843 (11-23-1843)
Edgemon, Nancy to David Walker 12-20-1841 (12-23-1841)
Edgman, Maryann to Abraham Clark 11-9-1840 (11-12-1840)
Edington, Mahaly to Wiley Gibson 5-22-1851
Edwards, Adaline to Joseph Romines 1-17-1843 (1-18-1843)
Edwards, Celia J. to Pleasant Myers 12-8-1862 (12-10-1862)
Elder, Clara to James W. Gresham 10-19-1865

Meigs County Brides

Elder, Mary to James H. Hewkirk 11-27-1842
Elder, Sarah to G. W. Houseley 5-9-1839
Eldridge, Luisa A. to C. W. Shamblin 9-6-1860 (9-18-1860)
Eldridge, Sarah to John McClanyhan 8-21-1865
Elis, Angeline to David? Miller 12-23-1845
Elison, Elenor to John Ford 10-24-1849 (10-25-1849)
Elison, Elizabeth to W. S. Maples 9-6-1849
Elkin, Larky to W. J. Young 8-31-1850
Ellis, Katharine to Wm. P. Gourley 3-14-1843
Ellis, Malissa J. to Cornelius Hafley 10-16-1854
Emery, Susan to Julius Hacker 11-15-1844
Emory, Racheal to Aron Grey 9-19-1857 (9-21-1857)
Emry, Nancy E. to John Massey 1-28-1856
Fairbanks, Eleanor to William Hall 9-22-1847
Fairbanks, Emeretta to James Madison Robeson 9-2-1846 (9-3-1846)
Falls, Abby J. to Joseph Bunch 9-27-1859 (9-28-1859)
Falls, Polly Ann to Grimes Bankston 2-17-1844
Farmer, Emily E. to Isaac J. Casey 6-13-1858 (6-17-1858)
Farmer, Sarah to Hosea H. Williams 4-19-1838 (5-24-1838)
Faro, Bethena to Washington Jones 10-13-1851
Farrar, Sarah E. to Geo. W. Gwinn 3-27-1854
Farrow, Polly to William Moore 4-29-1843
Fike, Dilla to Eli F. Mouncy 11-28-1848 (11-30-1848)
Filyan, Elizabeth to John Haney 8-30-1853
Fine, Susan to Wm. Langford 7-3-1856
Fitch, Catharine to Thomas Fitch 10-12-1865
Fitch, Edy W. to John Fitch 3-9-1847
Fitch, Mary to Isaac H. Conduff 12-25-1851
Fitch, Mary Ann to Andrew Eakin 11-13-1850
Fitch, Millie to Martin Haman 8-29-1855
Fitchjerls, Permelia to Francis M. Shiflet 8-2-1865
Floyd, Elisabeth to Squire Ford 9-30-1848 (10-1-1848)
Foar, Sarah to John W. Bandy 6-29-1865
Fooshee, Elizabeth to James E. Fikes 10-7-1845 (10-9-1845)
Fooshee, Elizabeth A. to John Duckworth 11-7-1863 (11-8-1863)
Fooshee, Mary to James Briggs 4-10-1850
Fooshee, Nancy to William Duckworth 8-9-1851
Ford, Eliza to Thomas Renfrow 12-13-1844
Ford, Elizabeth to Nathan Pelfrey 2-9-1841 (2-11-1841)
Ford, Jenny to Elkanah Rowden 5-23-1851
Ford, Mary to Josie Rowden 1-6-1848
Ford, Mary T. to Aquilla Farmer 5-24-1845 (5-25-1845)
Ford, Ruth to Thomas Cawood 12-22-1841 (12-25-1841)
Ford, Ruthy E. to Luck? M. King 12-23-1857
Ford, Sarah to Thos. Cawood 1-5-1854
Ford, Sarah to James M. Steen 8-10-1846 (8-13-1846)
Forde, Catharine J. to James Cunningham 5-2-1861 (5-5-1861)
Forde, Mahaley to James Massey 9-18-1846
Fore, Patience to David N. Newcom 2-6-1864 (2-7-1864)
Forrest, Mary to Tinsley Williams 9-19-1851

Meigs County Brides

Forsythe, Margaret to Alcander A. B. Craighead 4-19-1856
Four, Margret to John M. Hawser 12-31-1864
Fowler, Frances Ann to John Williams 11-12-1861 (10-13-1861)
Fox, Sarah to T. J. Martin 5-11-1844
Francisco, E. M. to Seth Atchley 2-18-1840 (3-2?-1840)
Francisco, Mart E. to Alfred Fitzgerald 1-21-1854
Francisco, Mary J. to Noah Aloon? 9-1-1845
Francisco, Nancy Ann to J. G. Johnson 11-17-1855
Francisco, Sarah A. to James H. Moore 8-15-1841
Frees?, Rebecca to Stephen Maner 5-21-1840
Frie, Malinda to henry Bard 4-2-1838
Frost, Lucinda to Andrew J. Seabourn 7-18-1849 (7-21-1849)
Fuller, Nancy to Coffield Tillery 7-14-1839
Fullington, Elizabeth to Elias Shoat 10-30-1844
Fyke, Elizabeth to Lehu Phillips 1-7-1840
Galloway, Annis M. to Waller L. Rothwell 12-6-1848 (12-7-1848)
Gamble, Catharine to Clinton Norman 1-25-1864 (1-26-1864)
Gamble, Charity A. to Joseph N. Wit 8-18-1849 (8-23-1849)
Gamble, Margaret J. to James M. Campbell 1-18-1847 (1-21-1847)
Gamble, Mary A. to W. R. Davis 2-22-1860
Gannay, Scyntha to W. B. Rigg 6-10-1852
Garrow, Eliza J. to Coffield Tillery 9-30-1851
Geiron, Abagail to Jacob Ray 10-30-1838
Geno, Louisa Jane to James W. More 10-30-1846
George, Sarah A. to Wm. Medley 3-18-1853
Gerl, Irena to James H. Ward 4-14-1842 (6-7-1842)
Gerrald, Emilin F. to Francis D. Okelly 11-14-1839
Gess, Fisha to Masoner Gross 12-26-1850
Gibson, Belinda to Morgan Bryan 12-11-1851
Gibson, Elizabeth to Wm. Wan 1-23-1845 (4-7-1845)
Gibson, Louisa to A. H. Butler 10-21-1857 (10-22-1857)
Gibson, Matilda to Jacob J. Butler 11-28-1849 (11-29-1849)
Gibson, Nancey Jane to Archable McCable 10-30-1848 (11-3-1848)
Gilbraith, Sarah Jane to Jno. M. Defriese 9-23-1865 (9-24-1865)
Gilbreath, Eliza J. to William Bracket 10-21-1845 (10-22-1845)
Ginett, Narcissa to Andrew Fox 2-4-1846
Gipson, Mary E. to James H. Knight 8-30-1865 (9-2-1865)
Goalden, Elizabeth to William Pharriss 6-18-1840
Godsey, Nancy A. to James Keziah 5-20-1857
Godsey, Sarah Ann to Thomas Hunter 11-19-1842 (11-20-1842)
Godsey, Sarah E. to A. L. Cross 11-26-1863
Goforth, Mahalda to Paul Bunch 12-22-1849 (12-23-1849)
Goley, Rebecca to John Helton 6-12-1850
Golloway, Eliza M. to John M. Albert 9-4-1845
Gorley, Levina P. to Thos. Blevins 6-13-1839 (7-1-1839)
Gourley, Clarissa to John Seaver 4-11-1846
Gourley, Maryann to Simon McGinnis 11-8-1838 (12-25-1838)
Gourley, Sarah F. to Benjamin F. Beeson 7-16-1844
Gray, Nancy to John Hatfield 10-24-1838
Green, Larena to A. H. McCall 9-4-1841 (9-5-1841)

Meigs County Brides

Green, Nancy to Levy Bradey 12-22-1841 (12-25-1841)
Green, Sarah Jane to William Johnson 10-18-1848 (10-19-1848)
Green, Sariah to James Franks 9-17-1849 (9-20-1849)
Green, Vesta M. (Emily?) to James M. Black 10-1-1851
Greenway, Emaline F. to Luke Richards 5-22-1854
Gregory, Mary to Lesley Myres 11-23-1857 (11-24-1857)
Gregory, Matilda J. to Leander M. Johnson 6-24-1858 (6-25-1858)
Gregory, Sarah Jane to Jos. C. Milts 10-2-1855
Gregory, _____ to Sterling Shelton 3-10-1840
Griffin, Iseller Ann to Anderson Griffin 7-23-1842 (7-24-1842)
Griffith, E. A. C. to E. H. Mathis 3-1-1858
Griffith, Salina to John L. Baldwin 3-10-1847 (3-11-1847)
Grigary, Mary to Lesley Myres 11-23-1857
Grigery, Elizabeth E. to W. Maberry 5-28-1842 (5-29-1842)
Grigsby, Martha J. to Thos. J. Defriese 6-5-1854
Grigsby, Nancy R. to Thomas C. Jordan 4-11-1844
Grisby, Elize to Clayton Miller 4-14-1851
Grissum, Peggy to Carter Young 9-26-1838 (9-27-1838)
Gross, Catherine to James Witt 9-16-1856
Gross, Margaret C. to Maximillian Conner 1-2-1855
Grubb, Julia to Daniel Wamack 2-10-1859 (2-13-1859)
Guess, Mary to Francis Gross 1-20-1848
Guinn, Elizabeth to Gilbert Munsey 5-19-1855
Guinn, Kisiah to Jacob Slauter? 1-13-1858 (1-14-1858)
Guinn, Malinda H. to William J. Abel 5-21-1850
Guinn, Martha L. to Calvin C. Robeson 4-29-1850
Guinn, Matilda to William Buster 12-31-1846
Guinn, Rachael to W. B. Adams 3-7-1851
Guinn, Sarah to James Smith 4-11-1850
Hagen, Susan to Andrew Farmer 9-19-1838 (9-20-1838)
Hague, Elizabeth C. to Wm. E. Gibson 9-11-1842
Hague, Sarah J. to Daniel Wan 5-13-1839 (6-6-1839)
Hail, Lucinda to Demsey Crow 6-11-1840
Hainy, Betsy to James Morgan 2-1-1847 (2-2-1847)
Hale, Lousey to Burrow Buckner 4-17-1858 (4-18-1858)
Hall, Rebeca to John Brooks 5-30-1840 (5-31-1840)
Hamilton, Rebecca to Larkin Buttram 2-27-1856
Hammons, Elnoa to James Ford 12-21-1854
Haney, Margaret to John Marshall 12-30-1851
Haney, Mary to William Rineheart 4-13-1858
Harp, Ailsey to William Collins 4-29-1856
Harpe, Elizabeth to W. J. Gaskey 2-20-1849
Harrid, Elizabeth to John Ashburn 10-24-1844
Harris, Adeline to John H. Haney 12-9-1864
Harvey, Elizabeth to William Griffen 9-18-1843 (9-19-1843)
Harvey, Phebe to Samuel Davis 11-5-1842 (11-6-1842)
Harvey, Vina to Calvin Mantooth 9-7-1844
Hatfield, Katherine to Thomas J. Hicks 11-22-1845
Haweson, Elizabeth to Thomas Moore 4-11-1854
Haynes, Matilda to James Dabney 10-7-1851

Meigs County Brides

Hayslett, Aslerene to Anderson Hunter 11-7-1843 (11-8-1843)
Heaton, Nancy to John R. Holmes 1-16-1855
Helton, Eliza Emeline to John Young 12-7-1847 (12-9-1847)
Hembree, Nancy to John Kerr 11-9-1854
Hembree, Susan to Abner Dotson 7-28-1846
Heney, Loucinda to G. T. Smith 1-17-1860 (1-18-1860)
Herrid, Sarah to Franklin Pierce 8-28-1845
Hickey, Amanda A. to Robert L. Weir 9-11-1851
Hill, Katharine to Green C. M. Gregory 1-9-1846 (1-21-1846)
Hill, Polly to Wm. Duckworth 3-7-1839
Hill, Rebecca to William Smith 12-14-1843
Holingsworth, Polly E. to (name illegible) 11-11-1859 (11-12-1859)
Hollamon, Elizabeth to P. L. Atchley 6-16-1863 (6-17-1863)
Holloman, Hannah to John M. Alford 4-13-1847
Holloman, Nancy to James Roark 10-6-1851
Holloman, Polly Jane to Arlander D. Alfred 4-7-1853
Holmes, Mary to Charles Prater 9-15-1838 (9-18-1838)
Homes, Mahalia to Thomas Blanton 3-2-1839 (3-7-1839)
Horrid, Matilda to Henry Price 4-15-1851
Hosuer, Sarah to James Burgess 1-14-1851
Hounshell, M. M. to L. L. Wear 7-19-1840
Hounshell, NSancy A. to Jonathan Wood 5-23-1844
Houpt, Margaret to Samuel Hardy 10-2-1850
Houser, Frances to William A. Reynolds 5-28-1849 (6-1-1849)
Houser, Frances to Wm. A. Reynolds 5-28-1840 (1-1-1841?)
Houser, Mary Jane to Elgin Brighwell 10-24-1850
Houser, Nancy to Gainum Brighwell 9-24-1850
Houser, Nancy R. to Thomas P. Tilly 2-4-1860 (2-5-1860)
Housley, A. E. to B. F. Webb 9-5-1865
Howard, Cyntha Ann to John Slaughter 6-15-1858? (6-16-1858?)
Howard, Elisebeth J. to Josiah Dolin 10-22-1857
Howard, Martha to William Farless 3-13-1862 (3-14-1862)
Howard, Sarah K. to William Wright 7-26-1862 (7-27-1862)
Howser, Elizabeth J. to Thomas G. Bonner 7-16-1861 (7-17-1861)
Hudson, Eliza to Spencer Adkins 5-18-1860 (5-20-1860)
Hudson, Mary to Francis M. Benton 7-10-1840 (7-12-1840)
Huff, Mary J. to James Sv.? Lillard 10-17-1847
Huff, Matilda to Thomas M. Gant 9-28-1857
Huff, Nancy Jane to William Lovelese 1-23-1859
Hufner, Elizabeth to Justice Edwards 10-27-1838 (10-28-1838)
Hughs, Mary to G. W. Click 4-4-1839
Huie(Hill?), Eleanor E. to William F. Pierce 9-15-1846 (9-16-1846)
Hunter, Dorcas A. to W. C. Hutchison 10-20-1850
Hunter, Elizabeth to Wm. Ingle 10-16-1855
Hunter, Esther C. to Mathew Kelley 12-28-1865
Hunter, Harret M. to Thomas Miller 9-26-1849 (10-4-1849)
Hunter, Marietta to Joshua L. Smith 10-26-1865
Hunter, Martha to John Dearmon 4-2-1851
Hunter, Sarah to S. S. Barrett 10-16-1865 (10-17-1865)
Hurt, Peggy to M. Furbunks 7-16-1839 (7-18-1839)

Meigs County Brides

Hutcherson, Mary A. to Robert E. Schoolfield 7-5-1849
Hutchinson, Sarah to Burton Holman 12-24-1844 (1-3-1845)
Hutdon, Mitilda F. to John F. Jaquiss 10-10-1851
Hutsell, Hester V. to John T. Maupin 6-10-1864 (6-12-1864)
Hutson, Nancy to Wilie O. Martin 1-31-1844
Hutton, Mary J. to Thos. T. Robinson 1-30-1865
Hymes, Susan to Joseph Collins 8-2-1864
Ingle, Polly to Emanuel Rhinehart 7-17-1844
Inman, Lurenna to Andrew Stuart 2-18-1843 (2-19-1843)
Irvin, Hannah J. to Henry R. Price 5-27-1862
Iseley, Elizabeth to David Wills 3-7-1843
Iseral, Kisiah to John Chapman 5-23-1855
Isley, Nancy to Nicodemus Ward 5-29-1843 (7-12-1843)
Isom, Serena to Benj. Bishop 1-4-1853
Jackson, Mary Jane to Ruben Cash 5-23-1853
Jenkins, Lucinda Jane to Nathan Colbaugh 2-17-1855
Johns, Cylva Jane to Joshua Starnes 7-26-1851
Johns, Nancy Ann to John L. Stanley 8-25-1854
Johns, Narcis to Henry Storris 1-11-1861 (1-13-1861)
Johnson, Catharine E. to William H. Hunter 6-14-1842 (6-16-1842)
Johnson, Elizabeth A. to Wm. Bolen 12-13-1863
Johnson, Elizabeth A. to Wm. H. Ferguson 11-24-1863
Johnson, Hariet G. to J. M. Butler 4-7-1845
Johnson, Mary to Jacob Williams 11-12-1861 (11-14-1861)
Johnson, Mary T. to John P. Hunter 1-5?-1842
Johnson, Prudence to John E. Carter 10-20-1857 (10-22-1857)
Johnson, Sarah to John M. Brown 12-10-1855
Johnson, Sarah to James H. Keyton 8-12-1865
Johnston, Malinda to Avery Hanner 4-26-1856
Jolley, Loucinda to Wilson Baker 12-20-1850
Jolley, Mahala to Jas. H. Jackson 11-2-1865
Jones, Betsey to John Fry 8-13-1856
Jones, Charity to Henry Williams 11-11-1864
Jones, Dicey Ann to Alexander Tharpe 2-24-1849 (2-25-1849)
Jones, Emeline to Daniel P. Atchley 1-20-1859 (1-21-1859)
Jones, Huldah to Joseph Stuart 2-10-1842 (2-11-1842)
Jones, M. to Wm. jr. McCarroll 7-13-1839 (7-16-1839)
Jones, Marthy M. to Benjamin F. McKenzie 9-9-1847
Jones, Nancy A. to George M. Simson 12-15-1852
Jones, Sarah to William Hackney 5-26-1851
Jones, Susan to Thomas Mee 9-2-1855
Keelin, Delpha to Samuel Wallin 6-27-1859 (9-3-1839)
Keeton, Artimissa M. to John Royster 11-30-1850
Kelley, Lourinda to Augustin Lillard 10-10-1850
Keneda, Barbary to Isaac Widows 12-26-1850
Kenedy, Telitha to Isaac Moore 6-16-1857 (not executed?)
Kennedy, Patience to Owen Falls 9-14-1864
Kennon?, Susan to G. W. McKenzie 2-15-1844
Keywood, Margaret P. to James Maden 1-18-1860 (1-20-1860)
Kincannon, Charlotte to James E. Collins 2-15-1862 (2-16-1862)

Meigs County Brides

Kincannon, Craton J. to Robert B. Hunter 9-25-1854
King, Ann to Joseph Stewart 9-11-1839 (9-12-1839)
King, Mirian to Henry L. Spicer 1-5-1856
King, Nancy M. to Shadrack William 10-18-1850
King, Susan J. to William J. Spicer 8-11-1853
Kinnamond, M. to Madison B. Johnson 10-10-1838 (10-12-1838)
Kinnum, Mary to Wm. B. Elderd 10-23-1844 (10-24-1844)
Kitchens, Susan to John Billings 8-5-1865
Kith?, Margaret to Leonard Brooks 12-23-1841
Kitten, Susan to William Miller 8-30-1838
Knight, Elizabeth to Madison Massengill 8-29-1838 (8-30-18380
Knight, Julian to William Lewman 6-29-1840 (7-5-1840)
Knight, Maria to Wm. P. Edds 1-25-1840
Knight, Susanna to Joseph Jolley 3-9-1842 (3-11-1842)
Kuntz, Sidney C. to Greenberry Bunch 4-27-1859 (4-28-1859)
Landagan, Mary to George Mitchell 11-18-1846
Lane, Elizabeth to H. D. McClanahan 10-17-1856
Lane, Rachel C. to William D. Michael 12-2-1844
Lane, Sarah A. to Henry H. Dennis 8-9-1864 (8-11-1864)
Lankford, Cynthia to Joseph Brown 1-21-1858
Lankford, Polly Ann to Samuel Price 5-7-1844 (5-9-1844)
Lankford, Sarah to M. V. Prestwood 8-1-1857
Larrants, Carline to E. J. West 5-5-1860 (5-6-1860)
Lason, Catharine to Joseph Manir 2-5-1840
Laves, Elizabeth to Richardson Rhea 5-13-1846 (5-14-1846)
Lawrence, Harret to Columbus Brown 10-21-1851
Lawson, Anna to Thos. Stapleton 5-15-1841
Lawson, Beddy to Thos. Owen 10-29-1857
Lawson, Brilia to Thomas Owen 10-29-1857
Lawson, Caldona E. to Wm. J. Barrows 11-24-1863
Lawson, Dicy (Miss) to Allen Lawson 3-24-1838 (3-25-1838)
Lawson, Elizabeth to Rhuben J. Williams 10-8-1857
Lawson, Jane to Blackburn Orical 11-22-1845
Lawson, Katharine to Isam Lawson 7-1-1842
Lawson, Liza Jane to David Bennett 8-25-1854
Lawson, Louisa to Geo. Romins 12-31-1851
Lawson, Margaret to Edmond Lawson 8-5-1850
Lawson, Martha A. to James Stokes 12-9-1852
Lawson, Rachel to Wm. Watts 7-20-1855
Lawson, Susanna to John Blankenship 5-24-1854
Ledbetter, Eliza to Doctor Pharis 2-16-1842 (2-17-1842)
Ledbetter, Hulda C. to C. Baker 9-10-1864
Ledbetter, Louiza J. to Jonathan D. Howerton 7-23-1847
Ledford, Delila to Claudius Hail 11-26-1843
Lentz?, Mary C. to Matthew B. Stewart 4-26-1864 4-29?-1864)
Lewis, Angenire to John W. Cosby 12-17-1850
Lewis, Jane to James Mays 7-11-1842 (7-12-1842)
Lewis, Luvena to Richard Brown 12-15-1848 (12-16-1848)
Lewis, Polly to William Marshall 10-20-1846
Lewis, Sophia to Jeremiah Miller 9-2-1840 (9-12-1840)

Meigs County Brides

Lewis, Susan to F. Rockhold 10-2-1865
Lillard, Craton to Josiah Martin 1-12-1854
Lillard, Louisa E. to Besiah Frazur 9-1-1858
Lillard, Martha J. to Aaron King 4-9-1842
Lillard, Mary A. to John B. Boggess 8-1-1850
Lillard, Texas to Wm. Stewart 2-23-1861
Little, Sarah to John W. Smith 2-10-1842
Lock, Elizabeth C. to Reubin C. Collins 8-17-1849 (8-18-1849)
Lock, Martha to Mason McClanahan 8-3-1860 (8-5-1860)
Lock, Mary to Jesse A. Lewis 9-3-1849 (9-5-1849)
Lock, Rebecca to Nicholas Gibson 8-18-1848 (8-20-1848)
Locke, Malindar to John McClanahan 9-10-1851
Locke, Mary to Wm. Foster 3-29-1865 (3-30-1865)
Locke, Sarah A. to Wm. Casey ?-?-1850
Locke, Sarah Catharine to Marion Columbus Clark 12-14-1861 (12-15-1861)
Locke, Susan to Elzy Buttram 9-2-1847
Lockman, Mary? A. to John W. Webb 10-3-1865
Lockmiller, Elizabeth to Wm. Martin 1-24-1856
Lockmiller, Nancy to Andrew J. Slaughter 9-12-1863 (9-13-1863)
Long, Rosana to Nathan Calbough 2-15?-1860
Looney, Elizabeth to Lewis Hart 10-14-1841
Looney, Sarah Jane to Wm. F. Aikman 2-15-1854
Loony, Dolly to sJohn Warmack 11-7-1840 (1-1-1841)
Losson, Sarah to Samuel Losson 4-10-1843 (4-11-1843)
Lovelace, Sarah A. to William J. Murphy 4-13-1859 (4-14-1859)
Low, Tennessee to William Cronville 1-19-1861
Lowder, Elisabeth to Jacob Gufey 6-4-1840
Lumes, Mariah to John H. Lullman 7-29-1852
Maberry, Elizabeth to Samuel Snow 12-28-1843
Mabery, Martha to James Robinson 8-17-1842
Mahan, Ann to Elisha Moore 3-27-1860
Mahan, Elizabeth to Philip Pierce 2-19-1845 (2-20-1845)
Mahan, Malinda to James Atchley 12-15-1852
Malone, Elizabeth J. to Jacob Ingle 12-27-1860
Malone, Julia Ann to Maidson White 9-17-1853
Malone, Mythursda to Francis Bishop 8-26-1851
Maloney, Lucinda to William L. Greene 12-30-1865 (12-31-1865)
Man, Jane to Albert Hix 4-19-1845
Manerd, Susan to Harvey Roark 3-24-1847
Mapes, Mary to Thomas J. Price 10-19-1846 (10-25-1846)
Mapes, Pricey to James T. Price 1-16-1847
Mapes, Sariah to William Watson 8-9-1849
Marshall, Milly to John Coxey 1-15-1856
Marshall, Nancy to Thos. Iviline 1-1-1851
Martin, Elizabeth to Henderson Choate 11-28-1862
Martin, Mertha? to John M. Lillard 1-1-1860
Martin, R. J. to E. Bonner 4-4-1860 (4-5-1860)
Martin, Sarah to James Corvin 8-21-1845 (8-25-1845)
Martin, Sarah to E. Grubb 9-29-1856
Martin, Sarah to James E. Lillard 1-19-1860

Meigs County Brides

Martin, Sarah to Hiram L. Miller 1-2-1855
Martin, Sarah C. to James Buckner 10-4-1858
Mason, Martha E. to Charles Gamble 7-12-1856
Masoner, Elizabeth A. to Calvin B. Atkinson 12-27-1847 (12-30-1847)
Masoner, Margaret to Jeremiah McKenzie 12-24-1856
Masoner, Ruth E. to James Long 7-28-1842
Masoner, V. T. to Saml. F. Martin 11-20-1865 (11-22-1865)
Massengale, Sarah to Noah R. Atchley 10-25-1862 (10-26-1862)
Mathews, Narcisis to Thomas Falls 8-20-1857
Mathis, S. P. to Elias L. Wier 11-22-1838 (11-23-1838)
Matlock, Gemina to Albert Browder 12-21-1846 (12-24-1846)
Matthes, Sableeche to Henry Newbary 10-11-1854
Matthews, Emeline to Robert Dobson 7-12-1861 (7-14-1861)
Matthews, Martha L. to Jesse Carter 9-20-1858
Matthews, P. A. to Jno. McClanahan 5-2-1851
Mavity, Jane to Noah Perry 9-25-1847
Mavity, Mary Ann to Francis M. Sewell 10-5-1848
Mavity, Nancy to James N. Grice 7-6-1842 (7-8-1842)
Mavity, Susannah to John Clemons 7-8-1845
Mawin, Mary Adaline to Cager Jackson Brown 5-8-1854
May, Mary A. to William Singleton 12-4-1856
May, Nancy Ann to Wm. Singleton 12-4-1856
Mayfield, Elizabeth to Morgan Bracket 11-4-1841
McAdams, MSary to Philip Davis 4-24-1840 (4-26-1840)
McAdams, Melsina to William Alexander 1-6-1847
McAdams, Telitha to John Wood 10-1-1839 (10-3-1839)
McAdoo, Margaret J. to John H. Davis 12-11-1850
McAdoo, Nancy to John Colbaugh 8-20-1855
McCall, Angelina to Enoch Ladd 3-4-1839 (3-14-1839)
McCall, M. A. to A. L. McCain 7-19-1865 (7-20-1865)
McCall, Sarah to John T. Shahan 12-7-1865
McCallen, Emaly M. to Thomas Draper 10-28-1852
McCallen, Hetty Ann to Newton Peak 11-15-1839 (11-16-1839)
McCartney, Mary Ann to John M. Lillard 6-4-1844
McCartney, Sarah J. to R. M. Lillard 5-8-1844 (5-9-1844)
McClanahan, Caroline to John B. Campbell 1-21-1846
McClanahan, Jane to John Cooley 11-8-1860
McClanyhan, Mary E. to A. W. McComack 7-30-1865
McClaren, Sarah Ann to C. M. K.(Charles) Welch 12-25-1841 (12-26-18
McClellan, Elizabeth to Josiah Locke 9-19-1853
McClenahan, Malinda to William Bourk? 5-9-1838
McClure, Catharine to William Key 4-18-1849 (4-25-1849)
McClure, Elizabeth V. to Thomas R. Rogers 11-12-1845 *
McClure, Polly to Stephen Matlock 7-12-1847
McCollon, Eleanor J. to Thomas S. Farmer 1-24-1842 (1-27-1842)
McCorkle, Charlottie to Tiry Lawson 7-18-1848 (8-7-1848)
McCorkle, Elisha to Ashbery S. Lillard 9-30-1849 (10-1-1849)
McCorkle, Eveline to Ambrose W. Hodge 10-6-1847 (10-7-1847)
McCorkle, Loucinda to Francis Lillard 11-19-1853
McCorkle, Maneroy to J. G. Jinkins 1-24-1851

Meigs County Brides

McCorkle, Matilda to Joseph T. Haynes 2-10-1853
McCorkle, Vernein? to J. A. Howell 4-2-1860 (4-10-1860)
McCoy, Margaret to Alfred Brackins 1-2-1841 (1-3-1841)
McDaniel, Elender to Joseph Collins 11-6-1850
McDaniel, Lousa to Jacob S. Emmert 6-25-1853
McDaniel, Martha to Jesse Martin 6-9-1841
McDaniel, Mary J. to Wm. L. Holden 3-20-1865
McDaniel, Miry to Daniel G. Stockton 1-11-1855
McDowell, Rebecca to Emanuel Parsons 11-27-1843
McEwin, Nancy L. to Elisha D. Thompson 3-7-1853
McGee, Catharine to Samuel Price 5-30-1853
McGill, Elenor to John Roishr 9-19-1851
McGinnis, Caroline to Francis m. Royster 2-16-1858 (2-18-1858)
McKinley, Angeline to Andrew Hunter 8-1-1848
McKinson?, Mary A. to John N. Davis 12-30-1862
McKown, Nancy to Henry C. Vanzart 2-28-1848 (2-29-1848)
McMullen, Lavina to R. J. D. W. Allen 7-29-1847
McMullen, Marth to Leander Melton 8-15-1847
McNabb, Sarah E. to James Duckworth 17-17-1864
McNutt, Mary to Thomas Rhea 8-30-1838 (9-6-1838)
McRennels, Sarah to Nathaniel Watson 9-28-1847
McWinton, Rodey to Wm. Ray 12-27-1848 (12-29-1848)
Mckeown, Manervy J. to Felix Barnhart 12-18-1845
Meadaris, Nancy Caroline to John Baker 1-9-1850
Medaris, Rachel E. to Samuel Baker 4-25-1853
Medley, Nancy to Wm. Moore 9-22-1853
Melton, Elizabeth C. to Thomas Purdy 8-14-1850
Melton, Emily J. L. to Saml. Gorley 6-28-1839 (6-30-1839)
Melton, Matilda to Lilborn Molton 2-1-1865
Melton, Nancy to Wm. Rockhold 3-17-1840
Melton, Nancy Ann to John jr. Taff 7-25-1858
Melton, Sarah to John Vaughan 2-26-1840 (4-18-1840)
Mesner, Mahala to Willet P. Howser 4-13-1865
Miller, Angeline to Z. F. Brooks 2-16-1856
Miller, Charlotte J. to Thomas H. Kincannon 6-29-1844
Miller, Evaline to Wm. J. Vincent 1-12-1854
Miller, Liza Jane to Samuel Vincent 2-7-1854
Miller, Lucy to Thomas D. Pierce 7-7-1865 (7-22-1865)
Miller, Martha J. to Alexander Moore 1-20-1851
Miller, Mary to James Revis 1-16-1850
Miller, Matilda L. to Nathan jr. Qualls 2-3-1844 (2-5-1844)
Miller, Nancy to John W. Haynes 5-20-1852
Miller, Nancy to J. A. Houser 1-7-1851
Miller, Nancy L. to George W. Qualls 3-23-1844 (3-24-1844)
Miller, Parry to John T. White 7-10-1851
Miller, Tennepe to Jacob Zeigler 10-21-1851
Miller?, Elizabeth to Gene Fullington 8-7-1838
Milloway, Betsy Ann to Wm. Brackett 12-14-1856
Milloway?, Rebecca J. to William Brackett 9-21-1858 (9-30-1858)
Mills, Eliner J. to John H. Lewis 8-21-1851

Meigs County Brides

Mitchell, Elizabeth to Miles Alcley? 7-21-1845
Mitchell, Margaret to William Londagan 10-1-1846
Mitchell, Nancy to Jacob Knight 4-22-1841
Molton, Ammey Mardy to Daniel M. Clerk 9-17-1849 (9-20-1849)
Moody, M. V. to O. A. Moody 7-30-1860 (7-31?-1860)
Moon, Martha Jane to Nicholas G. Givens 12-19-1855
Moore, Adaline to John G. Cash 8-4-1847
Moore, Barthena to John sr. Ingles 12-21-1843
Moore, Catharine to Franklin Genow 8-2-1848 (8-3-1848)
Moore, Louisa to Wallace Malone 11-2-1843
Moore, Malinda to Saml. G. Tankersley 6-13-1863
Moore, Mary to Wm. Maynor 12-30-1841
Moore, Mary Ann to John J. O'Neal 7-23-1844 (7-30-1844)
Moore, Nancy to James Greaves 4-13-1858 (5-22-1858)
Moore, Nancy to James F. Richardson 12-29-1847
Moore, Pheaby to John W. Smith 9-15-1838 (10-5-1838)
Moore, Roena to John Hunter 12-25-1849
Moore, Ruth J. to A. S. Wassum 2-20-1860 (2-23-1860)
Moore, Sarah to George W. Gaddy 6-19-1858 (6-24-1858)
More, Elvire to Abner Myers 12-30-1849 (12-31-1849)
Morelan, H. R. to Jesse Johns 3-14-1845 (3-17-1845)
Moreland, Martha to Isaac Cookson 4-15-1848
Morison, Mary J. to Timothy H. McCarty 3-6-1846 (3-10-1846)
Moss, Pasposia to Charles Richards 11-25-1854
Moss, Passea to Chas. Richards 11-25-1853
Moyers, Eleanor to Robert Simpson 4-2-1846
Moyers, Rebecca to Henry A. Lunsford 2-14-1846 (2-19-1846)
Moyers, Rutha to David Singleton 11-23-1838 (11-25-1838)
Mullens, Dorcas to Jesse Matthews 4-8-1842 (4-11-1842)
Mullins, Nancy Jane to Hugh Shoat 8-7-1851
Muncy, Viney to Henry L. Curton 6-9-1856
Munsey, Mary to Jeremiah Taylor 8-14-1863
Munsey, Nancy to Thomas J. Lawson 9-4-1844
Murphey, Mary E. to Wm. W. Brogden 11-29-1859
Murphy, Elizabeth to Samuel Blalock 11-24-1851
Murphy, Leane to Hugh Cash 12-21-1854
Murphy, Mary Ann to John Blythe 11-18-1854
Myers, M. E. to J. P. W. Cantrell 3-16-1863 (3-19-1863)
Myons, Eliza to Wiley G. Lunsford 2-11-1847
Myres, Lidda to Philo Corvin 11-18-1857 (11-24-1857)
Myres, Lidda to Philow Corvin 11-18-1857
Nance, Martha to Daniel Newman 4-1-1851
Neel, Mary to James McAdams 7-11-1843
Neil, Bethena to John Newman 12-5-1857 (12-6-1857)
Neil, Louisa to Levi F. Stewart 9-4-1860
Neil, Mahala R. to J. H. Boggess 1-31-1859 (2-3-1859)
Neil, Mary J. to James Thomas 2-15-1853
Neil, Sarah E. to Abraham Denton 3-27-1865 (3-29-1865)
Nelson, Elizabeth to Jacob Kizer 7-26-1860
Nelson, Mary D. to J. L. Hyde 1-21-1865

Meigs County Brides

Newkirk, Phereby to John L. Green 9-19-1842 (9-20-1842)
Newman, Mary to Philip Cooley 4-29-1863
Newman, Mary to Thomas Lewis 6-4-1859 (6-5-1859)
Newman, Nancy E. to John Bennett 12-6-1864
Newman, Vina to Albert Fairchild 12-11-1864
Nidiffer, Lucinda to David A. Moore 1-11-1840
Nite, Nancy to John Nite 4-21-1850
Norman, Hetty Ann to Dillard C. McMillen 11-4-1841
Norman, Mary J. to Samuel M. Wamack 10-6-1862 (10-5?-1862)
Norman, Vilena C. to Cyrus C. Hutcheson 4-13-1864
O'Neal, Mary to Washington Tims 8-19-1848 (8-20-1848)
Oleinger, Mary to James Burchfield 9-15-1860 (9-16-1860)
Overshultz, Malinda to John D. Bishop 12-10-1853
Owen, Dicy Ann to Samuel Jones 5-22-1846
Owen, Martha A. to A. J. Lawson 10-4-1865
Owen, Mary Ann to Benjamin F. Grigsby 8-9-1851
Owen, Nancy E. to John H. Fisher 10-13-1860 (10-14-1860)
Owen, Nancy Lovisa to John R. Tuell 9-6-1855
Owens, Elizabeth Ann to Ezekiel Marshall 4-6-1844
Owens, Margret to William C. Weitt? 10-20-1860 (10-21-1860)
Padgitt, Hetty to George W. Hale 3-10-1864
Paine, Matilda T. to William Eawin 7-20-1848 (7-23-1848)
Parton, N. J. to Wm. Myers 9-20-1864
Patterson, Jennie K. to Ethen Allen 12-25-1865 (12-26-1865)
Patterson, S. A. to A. G. Taff 12-19-1857 (12-20-1857)
Paul, Jane to George Becknell 6-23-1864
Paul, Marthy to Geo. Fooshee 8-2-1851
Paul, Mary A. to John H. Hood? 11-22-1864
Payne, Kiziah to Jackson Sliger 1-5-1858
Payne, Susan M. to Saml. Knox 7-11-1863
Peace, Sarah A.? to O. B. Harris 6-2-1864
Pearce, Elizabeth to Frederic H. Ford 10-16-1841
Pearce, Mary Jane to John Murphy 12-11-1864
Peirce, July Ann to Harvey McKenzie 10-17-1849 (10-18-1849)
Peirce, Sarah M. to Henry M. Miller 8-15-1849 (8-16-1849)
Peirce, Sariah to Moses H. Edds 9-24-1849 (9-25-1849)
Pellason, Louisa to B. F. Starns 10-14-1851
Perry, Celia to Leven S. Coffey 12-24-1844
Perry, Mary to Thomas C. Stokes 1-15-1846
Petitt, Eliza to Charles McCarell 2-5-1842 (2-6-1842)
Pettitt, Luovina to James Burley 7-15-1843
Pettitt, Polly to Martin Lawson 11-22-1844
Pharriss?, Nancy to Wm. Crudgington 5-13-1838
Philip, Lucinda to Pollard Edgman 3-7-1859 (3-22-1859)
Philips, Drucilla to Wm. Mabary 2-18-1843
Philips, Elizabeth J. to William Fitch 8-4-1847
Philips, Kisiah to Kimball Edgeman 10-15-1855
Philips, Mary to John Keed 12-6-1844 (12-12-1844)
Phillips, Sarah E. to Jacob Webb 8-16-1864 (8-18-1864)
Philpot, M. to Henry J. Hodge 10-12-1838

Meigs County Brides

Philpott, Mary to Thomas Sparks 5-31-1843
Pierce, Elizabeth to John Price 10-28-1851
Pierce, Jane to Simon Sharp 8-23-1857
Pierce, Margaret D. to Jesse Hamilton 9-11-1865
Pierce, Martha E. to Martin L. Boyd 3-5-1856
Pierce, Prudy Ann to John K. Edds 3-27-1845
Poe, Elizabeth to William Rineheart 11-8-1860
Poplin, Roddy to Harvey Richardson 12-8-1859
Porter, E. T. to Thomas McKnight 12-24-1861 (12-25-1861)
Porter, Maryann to David C. Dempsey 9-12-1842
Porter, Sarah to T. J. Leonard 12-21-1850
Powers, Martha A. to Henry Collins 3-16-1864 (3-24-1864)
Powers, Sarah G.? to Robt. Atchley 6-3-1859 (6-4-1859)
Presswood, Manervy to Martin Cranfield 7-12-1860
Prewitt, Mary Ann to Solomon Harden 6-12-1845
Price, Elizabeth Ann to Jackson Smith 7-6-1862
Price, Evaline T. to B. F. Thomas 1-29-1865 (1-30-1865)
Price, Jane to Sylvester Corder 9-27-1864
Price, Louisa to Jacob Tillery 7-31-1845
Price, Louisa E. to Wm. G. Overton? 10-5-1841 (10-7-1841)
Price, Louisa J. to W. L. Wood 11-14-1864
Price, Martha to Isac Butten 12-26-1851
Price, Martha J. to Robert Simpson 8-4-1864 (8-5-1864)
Price, Mary to Thomas Cranfill 6-21-1863
Price, Mary Ann to Cage Low 7-3-1845
Price, Minerva to Joseph Mapes 7-29-1846
Price, Nancy to Wm. Buster 1-17-1839 (1-20-1839)
Price, Rachel to Wm. Lawson 6-8-1854
Price, Sarah to A. Sweatman 8-10-1847
Price, Sarah Jane to Sylvester Corder 12-30-1864
Purdy, Martha to Henry Long 7-5-1854
Quiett, Caroline to Anderson Blevins 12-30-1847 (8-7-1848)
Quiett, Elinder to John M. McDaniel 12-4-1850
Raby, Franky to Samuel Bly 12-25-1865 (12-28-1865)
Ragland, Elizabeth W. to Nelson C. Redman 10-14-1841
Ramsey, Elizabeth to James Fox 2-19-1846
Ramsey, Milia to Stephen J. McClannahan 5-2-1844 (5-15-1844)
Ramsey, Nancy to Isaac Colwell 6-2-1853
Ramsey, Sarah to Wm. Farbank 1-26-1839 (2-1-1839)
Ray, Anner to WM. Hair 1-27-1840
Reace, Eliza to John N.? McKain 12-20-1865 (12-25-1865)
Reace, Mary to Hankins Daniel 10-7-1851
Read, Sarah A. to Samuel Deatherige 7-6-1850
Rector, Sarah Ann to James Hany 5-27-1847
Redmon, Mahala E. to Nelson Monger 6-13-1856
Redmond, Mary A. to James T. Johnson 12-8-1865 (12-10-1865)
Reed, Eliza J. to Thomas Bowling 11-2-1862
Reed, Judy Lovisa to James Neil 8-8-1848 (8-10-1848)
Reed, Lones to William Myers 12-17-1847 (12-18-1847)
Reed, Nancy A. to Charles Gamble 2-17-1847 (2-18-1847)

Meigs County Brides

Reims, Martha to F. M. Moore 10-6-1840
Rence, Nermawey Law to Edman Forde 1-27-1851
Renfroe, Naoma to Isaiah Allen 12-25-1832
Renfrow, Polly to Samuel Baker 8-26-1850
Renow, Lavina to James M. Hancock 10-9-1838
Rew, Elizabeth to Samuel Woody 4-3-1850
Reynolds, Matilda to Isaac McKeown 11-30-1842 (12-1-1842)
Reynolds, Susanna to James M. Owens 8-14-1849 (8-16-1849)
Rhineheart, Rebeccah to John Price? 6-28-1838 (6-29-1838)
Rhinheart, Ann to Wm. Thorp 9-20-1841 (1-1-1849?)
Rhodes, Elizabeth to Jno. N. Ball 7-2-1863 (7-3-1863)
Rice, Elizabeth to Alexander Correll 8-14-1851
Rice, Lockey to Wm. M. Correll 9-15-1854
Rice, Mahala to Charles Smith 7-20-1858
Rice, Mary to M. A. White 9-2-1851
Rice, Susan to Wm. H. Dearmon 6-29-1847 (7-1-1847)
Richards, C. E. to W. A. Myers 9-15-1857 (9-20-1857)
Richards, Dicey to James Bell 4-8-1854
Richards, Edith S. to B. M. Frew? 7-17-1862
Richards, Lovisa J. to James J. Floyd 9-16-1848 (9-17-1848)
Richards, Mahuldah R. to Stephen Pane 2-24-1842
Richards, Polly M. to William Bolin 10-29-1848
Richardson, Eliza J. to Calvin Rice 11-5-1845 (11-6-1845)
Rigg, Jane to James E. Collins 9-13-1843 (9-14-1843)
Rigg, Martha to H. Whitmore 2-9-1860
Rigg, Minerva Jane to Andrew J. Mavity 1-17-1856
Riggins, Nancy to George Hughs 7-2-1858 (7-20-1858)
Rivers, Martha to Creed Walker 7-6-1840 (7-7-1840)
Roads, Sarah J. to J. V.? Moore 8-3-1857
Roark, Mary Ann to Crisley Hackler 10-6-1840
Roark, Nancy to Joshua E. Witten 11-26-1846 (11-30-1846)
Roberds, Susan Jane to Creed F. Marshall 9-16-1853
Robertson, Frances to Geo. W. Ahart 9-24-1850
Robeson, Mary (Nancy) to Wm. Redmon 4-4-1838 (4-19-1838)
Robeson, Temperance M. to John E. McKelpin 6-17-1849 (6-19-1849)
Rodis, Louisa to Benjamin Cash 3-18-1846 (3-19-1846)
Rogers, Annas to Joseph Pervine 7-28-1860 (7-29-1860)
Rogers, Dinely to Eli Colvin 7-11-1846
Rogers, Ellen Tennessee to Granville C. Sandusky 9-3-1856
Rogers, July Ann to Wm. P. Richardson 1-4-1844
Rogers, Mahala to A. R. Snider 10-22-1850
Rogers, Mary J. to Nathan Richardson 11-27-1845 (11-30-1845)
Rogers, Matilda to James H. Lock 6-20-1846
Rogers, Nancy to John Tillery 2-1-1845
Rogers, Sarah to Frederick Wirick 10-5-1841
Roork, Dicy to Jackson West 3-21-1843
Roork, Margaret to William Knox 2-24-1843
Rothwell, Malisy to Jacob Buster 10-17-1860
Rouden, Malinda to James Butler 5-29-1844
Rowden, Adaline to B. J. Paul 12-16-1856

Meigs County Brides

Rowden, Elizabeth to Joshua Renfroe 3-4-1850
Rowden, Emaline to James Correll 11-1-1856
Rowden, Mahala to Wm. L. Plank 12-4-1841
Rowden, Mary M. to James W. Paul 11-2-1853
Rowden, Sarah Armitz to John Moss 9-29-1853
Rowden, Susan to Ewell Johnson 12-22-1846 (12-23-1846)
Rowden, Susan to John R. Renfrow 1-3-1851
Rowden, Telitha C. to James M. George 10-30-1855
Royster, Caroline to Jonathan M. Collins 1-27-1849 (1-28-1849)
Royster, Elizabeth to Wm. A. Witt 7-30-1842 (7-31-1842)
Royster, M. A. to Saml. Buster 8-13-1839 (8-18-1839)
Runyan, Ann to Isaac R. Erwin 11-24-1860 (11-29-1860)
Runyan, Ava to William R. Erwin 11-24-1860 (11-27-1860)
Runyan, Malinda J. to Christopher T. Roberts 2-2-1864
Runyon, Penelope A. to E. G. McKenzie 1-13-1858 (1-16-1858)
Russell, Elizabeth A. to Wright S. Miller 8-12-1847
Russell, Susan to John M. Cox 12-1-1851
Sadler, E. R. to John Cliften 12-31-1843
Scott, Magana to James Millikin 5-5-1857
Scott, Mary Ann to John Cox 2-16-1848 (8-7-1848)
Sears, Dicy to Wm. Smith 11-24-1845 (11-26-1845)
Sears, Frankey to Leonard Huff 11-19-1845 (11-20-1845)
Selph, Eliza to William Moore 9-12-1848
Selvage, Louisa to Robert Tharp 8-15-1865
Sewell, Rebecca to Joseph L. Collins 11-30-1852
Sharp, Harriet C. to Darius Waterhouse 5-4-1846 (5-7-1846)
Sharp, Jane to Wright Smith 11-29-1843 (11-30-1843)
Sharp, Levina to Abijah Boggess 2-3-1851
Sharp, Mary to B. F. Locke 11-17-1840 (11-19-1840)
Sharp, Rachel to Isah Homes 6-12-1846
Sharp, Sarah Ann to G. M. Clementson 10-28-1854
Shears, Altamyra to Philip M. Blevins 9-5-1858
Shell, Elizabeth to Thomas Newman 4-25-1855
Shelton, Eliza to Edward Sharp 8-16-1842
Shelton, Lydia M. to John Shelton 4-7-1841 (4-8-1841)
Shelton, Martha to Joshua Lewis 3-2-1839 (3-3-1839)
Sherman, Elisabeth to John W. Dodson 1-31-1865
Shewbird, Nancy to Wm. Childres 9-17-1853
Shiflet, Mary Ann to Joseph Cofer 7-28-1842
Shiflet, Nancy J. to John Cofer 7-30-1845
Shiflett, Nancy J. to John Cofer 7-30-1845
Shiflett, Sarah to Andrew Campbell 11-10-1840 (11-12-1840)
Shipley, Barbara L. to Jacob Fitch 12-10-1864
Shiply, Betsy to John Calbough 12-15-1851
Shiply, Harriet E. to Jesse Witt 7-28-1860 (7-29-1860)
Simpson, Eda Caroline to Martin H. Stephens 4-13-1848
Simpson, Elisabeth to Richard Hicks 9-14-1857
Simpson, Elizabeth to Wm. Z. Gallion 7-25-1853
Simpson, Lydia to Henry Sligar 11-22-1846
Simpson, Sarah to Daniel McDowell 6-16-1838 (6-21-1838)

Meigs County Brides

Sims, Celia B. to Wm. R. Gemore? 7-6-1864 (7-7-1864)
Singleton, Ann to Luke P. Martin 7-30-1856
Singleton, Nancy to A. B. Michals 1-8-1846
Slaughter, Elizabeth M. to John Henson 8-18-1838 (8-21-1838)
Sligar, Sarah to James Sligar 10-1-1864 (10-2-1864)
Slinger, Vilety to James Taylor 12-14-1850
Small, Jane to Frederick M. Johnson 2-10-1846
Small, Mary E. to Robert Low 2-4-1860
Smith, Adda to W. S. Hughs 6-14-1857 (6-16-1857)
Smith, Angeline to Claibon? Norman 12-29-1862 (not executed)
Smith, Angeline to Jehu Poplin 4-26-1864
Smith, Elizabeth to Joseph R. Richards 6-30-1853
Smith, Elsira to R. J. D. W. Aller 8-24-1857 (8-25-1857)
Smith, Katharine to David Mitchell 4-6-1846
Smith, Malindy Jane to Abner Guinn 4-11-1850
Smith, Margaret to John Mitchell 10-15-1846
Smith, Martha to Wm. L. Ward 9-12-1864
Smith, Mary to Thomas Cox 3-19-1847
Smith, Rebecca to Lewis Benton 5-28-1849
Smith, Rebecca to Hiram Harred 2-9-1854
Snider, Sarah to James McKinnie 12-11-1851
Snow, Frances to John Smith 9-22-1838 (10-2-1838)
Snow, Polly to Jordan Smith 1-12-1842
Soils, Caroline M. to Robert Simpson 2-12-1861
Spradlin, Mary to J. A. Davis 1-13-1859 (1-14-1859)
Stanley, Mary to Sanford Adkins 1-29-1850
Stanley, Nancy to Asel C. Shamblin 1-9-1853
Stanley, Susan to Jonathan Isom 12-23-1850
Stanly, Lidia Ann to Wm. M. Childress 11-13-1841
Starnes, Sarah C. to P. J. Dean 12-22-1843 (12-24-1843)
Starnes, Sopha to Robert W. Myers 7-20-1853
Starns, Rebecca to Mardica Floyd 10-30-1852
Starns, Rosana to John Moore 11-12-1857
Stephens, Emly Jane to W. C. Watson 9-28-1852
Stephens, Susan to A. J. Prewett 5-30-1846 (5-31-1846)
Stepp, Martha to John Richardson 4-27-1857
Sterns, Sarah to Owen Martin 1-6-1844
Stewart, Leta B. to W. L. Grisby 8-3-1858
Stewart, Letitia Ann to Reuben McKenzie 6-2-1859
Stewart, Mary to Richard Taylor 12-11-1851
Stockton, Artemiza B. to John P. Redmon 1-6-1845
Stockton, Celia Jane to Henry P. Ward 9-9-1853
Stockton, Sarah Earnestine to Samuel Stockton 5-29-1850
Stokes, Celia to Jas. O. Jones 7-18-1855
Stokes, MSary to Isaac Hutchison 1-29-1840
Stokes, Martha to John Davis 5-29-1856
Stokes, Mary to James Revis 2-25-1854
Stone, Jane L. to Jonathan K. Chastian 8-21-1843
Stone, Lucy Ann to Elijah Atchley 9-27-1859
Stone, Parle to James A. Aikman? 7-19-1860

Meigs County Brides

Stout, Martha to James Pettitt 12-1-1841 (12-2-1841)
Stuart, M. to P. Miller 11-9-1843
Sulivan, Elizabeth to Delaney Trusler 2-25-1846 (2-26-1846)
Sulivan, Milbery to Elisha More 10-3-1848 (10-5-1848)
Sullivan, Martha to Martin Cunningham 1-25-1844
Sutherland, Eliz. to Jas. McNutt 10-8-1839
Sutherland, Mary to John Brandon 7-?-1858 (7-1-1858)
Swaggerty, Phebe E. to James Milligan 9-14-1861 (10-15-1861)
Swofford, Rebecca to John Sluter 2-29-1842
Sykes, Ann to John Rigsby 7-30-1856
Taff, Emily to Amedia Rice 10-1-1850
Taff, Margaret I. to James Doughty 5-19-1854
Taff, Martha E. to Rice Hughes 1-2-1840
Tally, Edy to James Fitch 1-13-1846
Tankersley, Elizabeth to Wm. H. Wilson 6-8-1861 (8-5-1861)
Tankersley, Susan to Andrew B. Kitchen 10-12-1854
Taylor, Lively to Henry McVoy 4-11-1846
Taylor, Lorinda to John Kelly 10-15-1840 (10-18-1840)
Taylor, Mary to Isaac Cross 11-24-1853
Taylor, Sophia to Wm. Childress 9-19-1841
Teague, Peggy to Philow Corvin 2-7-1845 (2-10-1845)
Thomas, Elizabeth to Moses Blevins 8-27-1839 (8-29-1839)
Thomas, Julia to Wm. Godsey 12-18-1840 (12-21-1840)
Thomas, Lucretia to William M. Lillard 10-22-1845
Thomas, Nancy to Alfred Cate 8-14-1845
Thomas, Sarah to VanBuren Copeland 4-7-1854
Thompson, Katharine to James Burcham 3-3-1847 (3-4-1847)
Thompson, Rebecca S. to Calloway Gresham 8-16-1845 (8-17-1845)
Thornberry, Mary to Jno. Hobbs 3-30-1839 (4-4-1839)
Tillerry, Rachel to John Atchley 7-27-1851
Tillery, Barbara A. to Miles V. Preswood 2-26-1845 (2-27-1845)
Tillery, Elender A. to Thomas Elsay 9-16-1840 (9-17-1840)
Tillery, Eliza J. to Lewis E. Shope 7-25-1865 (7-30-1865)
Tillery, Elizabeth to Pleasant M. Preswood 9-24-1844 (9-26-1844)
Tillery, Irena to W. J. Duckworth 5-8-1864
Tillery, L. to Thos. H. Lewy 7-14-1839 (7-15-1839)
Tillery, Mahala E. to Wm. Atchley 1-22-1856
Tillery, Margaret to Joseph H. Cote 9-1-1842
Tillery, Tennessee to James Atchley 6-25-1863 (6-26-1863)
Tilley, Permelie E. to Robert S. Gamble 1-25-1859
Todd, M. E. to E. R. Chattin 12-3-1849 (12-5-1849)
Tolbert, Lidian to James Hicks 4-27-1858
Towell, Nancie to Luke Martin 5-29-1851
Tuck, Mary to James Blythe 6-7-1854
Underwood, Nancy to Cyrus Quiett 4-17-1842
Vaughn, Annice to Pleaseant Miller 1-26-1853
Vaughn, Catharine to George W. Cate 3-27-1864
Vaughn, Mary to Milton E. Jameson 12-15-1846
Vernon, Martha A. E. to William D. Reynolds 8-6-1849 (8-9-1849)
Vetito, Sarah J. to William Jones 11-28-1844

Meigs County Brides

Voils, Luisa to William Roods 2-20-1861
Wade, Emily J. to Daniel Rivers 12-31-1846
Wadkins, Hariet J. to William Johnson 7-1-1844 (7-5-1844)
Walden, Lucinda to Aaron Smith 1-29-1839 (1-30-1839)
Walding, Mary to Elias Crisp 9-3-1838 (9-9-1838)
Walker, Nancy to Gainum Brightwell 12-29-1839
Walker, Ruth to Marion Home 4-13-1864
Walker, Sarah to John Watkins 9-20-1855
Wamac, Mary A. to Wm. C. Grubb 6-25-1853
Wamack, Jane to Saml. C. Allen 11-5-1861
Wamack, Melissa to John Benson 2-25-1864
Wamack, Sarah to James F. Pierce 3-1-1855
Wamack, Susanah to Thomas G. Bonner 3-21-1859
Wammack, Mary to John C. George 8-31-1850
Wammack, Sarah to Thomas J. Bonner 9-5-1850
Wan, Elizabeth to Michael W. Buster 12-24-1845 (12-25-1845)
Wan, Hannah to Henry Small 4-9-1846
Wan, Jane to Benjamin Hutson 9-4-1848 (9-5-1848)
Wan, Sarah to John Small 9-24-1845 (9-25-1845)
Wan, Sarah E. to James Baker 11-17-1857 (11-19-1857)
Ward, Polly to William Jolly 8-4-1849
Warrick, Mary Jane to A. B.? Smith 9-18-1844
Wassen, Nancy to B. F. Huff 12-20-1842 (12-22-1842)
Wasson, Elizabeth to Enoch Collins 7-28-1849 (8-9-1849)
Wasson, Sarah H. to Thomas P. Moore 6-22-1861
Watkins, Mary E. to G. W. Mathews 7-23-1842
Watson, Rachel to Isaac Butler 10-2-1857 (11-2-1857)
Webb, Mahala to Murphree H. Vaughn 10-31-1849 (11-1-1849)
Welchhance, Elizabeth to James Stone 3-18-1851
Welsh, Minerva to Wm. Childress 4-11-1863 (4-12-1863)
West, Betsy to Wm. Redman 9-12-1843
Whaley, Mary to John Jinkins 9-24-1850
Whaly, Vilet to _____ Peoples 10-13-1851
White, Emaline to Aron Vaughn 5-6-1860
White, Sarah to Joseph Perdy 12-13-1851
Whitmore, Elizabeth to Greene Williams 11-10-1862 (11-12-1862)
Whitmore, Louisa to John W. Williams 12-23-1852
Whitmore, Mary I. to Jos. H. Witt 10-29-1856
Whitson, Sariah to Isaac McDowell 2-31-1849 (1-1-1850)
Wilhelms, _____ to Jno. Tindel 9-1-1839 (9-12-1839)
Willes, Ruth to James Millicen 2-7-1854
Willhelms, Sarah to M. P. Howard 7-14-1861 (7-15-1860)
Williams, Abbigail to Robert Turner 11-12-1861 (11-20-1861)
Williams, Anna to Michael W. Coffey 4-6-1842 (4-7-1842)
Williams, Mary to Reuben E. Bandy 2-15-1840 (2-16-1840)
Williams, Nancy to Thos. Moore 1-23-1841 (4-5-1841)
Wilson, Clarrinza L. to Amos Broiles 7-1-1845
Wilson, Eleanor C. to Miles M. Broyles 5-20-1845
Wilson, Emily to Moses Kennedy 11-1-1841 (11-7-1841)
Wilson, Jane to Henry Barnhart 4-21-1847 (4-22-1847)

Meigs County Brides

Winton, Martha W. to Hugh Goddard 11-16-1847 (11-6?-1847)
Winton, Mary J. to John Ray 3-2-1849 (3-6-1849)
Winton, Mary J. to Elijah S. Smith 4-4-1844
Winton, Sarah S. to John H. Pickle 8-11-1845 (8-14-1845)
Witmps, Mary M. to W. J. Owny 12-25-1852
Witt, Emaline E. to Evander T. McCorkle 6-19-1860
Witt, Matilda to Avery Hannah 2-1-1842 (1?-3-1842)
Witt, Nancy to Wm. Gresham 9-13-1856
Witt, Sarah to A. B. Cate 1-22-1860
Witten, Lutitia to John H. Roark 10-18-1847 (10-21-1847)
Womack, Elizabeth to James M. Masoner 3-6-1861 (3-7-1861)
Wood, Celia A. to James M. Ford 4-25-1853
Wood, Jennetta to Nat? Witt 3-1-1860 (3-2-1860)
Wood, Martha J. to James H. Holt 7-16-1863
Woods, E. E. to Wm. K. Jinkins 2-24-1842
Woods, Elizabeth to George . Wilson 6-11-1842 (6-14-1842)
Woods, Jailey L. to Wm. E. Smith 5-2-1861 (5-2-1861)
Woods, Mary A. to George W. Hail 12-18-1845
Woods, Nancy E. to Richard Binyon 11-21-1850
Worick, Mary Ann to A. J. Brooks 1-9-1845 (1-12-1845)
Wren?, Jan T. to Jesse Derrick? 6-25-1838 (6-20?-1838)
Yeanas, Susan to William Redman 11-26-1857 (11-27-1857)
Yonas, Nancy to Bartly Lawson 1-29-1847
Yonas, Rebecca to John Owens 1-13-1847
Yonas, Rebecca to John Owens 1-7-1847
Young, Elisa Jane to Wm. Collins 10-15-1849
Young, Lousa to Hilliogabinous Davis 9-16-1853